playing in the dark

the william e. massey sr. lectures
in the history of american civilization
1990

toni morrison

playing in the dark

whiteness and the literary imagination

harvard university press

cambridge, massachusetts, and london, england

Lines from T. S. Eliot, "Preludes, IV," in *Collected Poems, 1909–1962*, copyright 1936 by Harcourt Brace Jovanovich, Inc., copyright © 1943, 1963, 1964 by T. S. Eliot, reprinted by permission of the publisher. Lines from William Carlos Williams, "Adam," in *Collected Earlier Poems*, copyright 1938 by New Directions Publishing Corporation, reprinted by permission of the publisher.

This book is printed on acid-free paper, and its binding materials have been chosen for strength and durability.

Library of Congress cataloging information at end of book

preface

Some years ago, in 1983 I believe, I read Marie Cardinal's *The Words To Say It*. More than the enthusiasm of the person who suggested the book, I was persuaded by the title: five words taken from Boileau that spoke the full agenda and unequivocal goal of a novelist. Cardinal's project was not fictional, however; it was to document her madness, her therapy, and the complicated process of healing in language as exact and as evocative as possible in order to make both her experience and her understanding of it accessible to a stranger. The narrative into which life seems to cast itself surfaces most forcefully in certain kinds of psychoanalysis, and Cardinal proves herself ideal in rendering this "deep story" aspect of her life. She has written several books, won the Prix International, taught philosophy, and, during her journey into health, admits that she always planned someday to write about it.

It is a fascinating book and, although I was skeptical at first of its classification as "autobiographical novel," the accuracy of the label quickly becomes apparent. It is shaped quite

as novels most frequently are with scenes and dialogue selec-
tively ordered and situated to satisfy conventional narrative
expectations. There are flashbacks, well-placed descriptive
passages, carefully paced action, and timely discoveries.
Clearly her preoccupations, her strategies, and her efforts to
make chaos coherent are familiar to novelists.

From the beginning I found one question insisting itself:
when precisely did the author know she was in trouble? What
was the narrative moment, the specular even spectacular scene
that convinced her that she was in danger of collapse? Less
than forty pages into the book she describes that moment,
her "first encounter with the Thing."

"My first anxiety attack occurred during a Louis
Armstrong concert. I was nineteen or twenty.
Armstrong was going to improvise with his trumpet,
to build a whole composition in which each note
would be important and would contain within itself
the essence of the whole. I was not disappointed: the
atmosphere warmed up very fast. The scaffolding and
flying buttresses of the jazz instruments supported
Armstrong's trumpet, creating spaces which were
adequate enough for it to climb higher, establish
itself, and take off again. The sounds of the trumpet
sometimes piled up together, fusing a new musical
base, a sort of matrix which gave birth to one precise,
unique note, tracing a sound whose path was almost
painful, so absolutely necessary had its equilibrium

and duration become; it tore at the nerves of those who followed it.

"My heart began to accelerate, becoming more important than the music, shaking the bars of my rib cage, compressing my lungs so the air could no longer enter them. Gripped by panic at the idea of dying there in the middle of spasms, stomping feet, and the crowd howling, I ran into the street like someone possessed."

I remember smiling when I read that, partly in admiration of the clarity in her recollection of the music—its immediacy—partly because of what leaped into my mind: what on earth was Louie playing that night? What was there in his music that drove this sensitive young girl hyperventilating into the street to be struck by the beauty and ravage of a camellia "svelte in appearance but torn apart inside"?

Enunciating that incident was crucial in the launching of her therapy, but the imagery that worked as a catalyst for her anxiety attack goes unremarked—by her, by her analyst, and by the eminent doctor, Bruno Bettelheim, who wrote both the Preface and the Afterword. None of them is interested in what ignited her strong apprehension of death ("I'm going to die!" is what she was thinking and screaming), of physical power out of control ("nothing could appease me. And so I continued to run"), as well as this curious flight from the genius of improvisation, sublime order, poise, and the illusion of permanence. The "one precise, *unique* note, tracing

a sound whose path was almost *painful,* so absolutely necessary had its *equilibrium* and *duration* become; it *tore at the
nerves* of those [other than Armstrong, apparently] who followed it" [italics mine]. Unbearable equilibrium and duration; nerve-wracking balance and permanence. These are
wonderful tropes for the illness that was breaking up Cardinal's life. Would an Edith Piaf concert or a Dvorak composition have had the same effect? Certainly either could have.
What solicited my attention was whether the cultural associations of jazz were as important to Cardinal's "possession" as
were its intellectual foundations. I was interested, as I had
been for a long time, in the way black people ignite critical
moments of discovery or change or emphasis in literature not
written by them. In fact I had started, casually like a game,
keeping a file of such instances.

The Louis Armstrong catalyst was an addition to this file,
and encouraged me to reflect on the consequences of jazz—
its visceral, emotional, and intellectual impact on the listener.
Later on in Cardinal's autobiography, another luminous
moment is described. But this one is not a violently physical
reaction to the art of a black musician; it is instead a conceptual response to a black, that is, nonwhite, figuration. The
author names the manifestation of her illness—the hal-
lucinatory images of fear and self-loathing—the Thing. In
reconstructing the origin of the powerfully repellent feelings
the Thing incites, Cardinal writes, "It seems to me that the
Thing took root in me permanently when I understood that
we were to assassinate Algeria. For Algeria was my real

mother. I carried her inside me the way a child carries the blood of his parents in his veins." She goes on to record the conflicting pain that war in Algeria caused her as a French girl born in Algeria, and her association of that country with the pleasures of childhood and budding sexuality. In moving images of matricide, of white slaughter of a black mother, she locates the origin of the Thing. Again, an internal devastation is aligned with a socially governed relationship with race. She was a colonialist, a white child, loving and loved by Arabs, but warned against them in relationships other than distant and controlled ones. Indeed, a white camellia "svelte in appearance but torn apart inside."

In Cardinal's narrative, black or colored people and symbolic figurations of blackness are markers for the benevolent and the wicked; the spiritual (thrilling tales of Allah's winged horse) and the voluptuous; of "sinful" but delicious sensuality coupled with demands for purity and restraint. These figures take shape, form patterns, and play about in the pages of the autobiography. One of her earliest realizations in therapy concerns prepubescent sexuality. When she understands and no longer despises this aspect of her self, Cardinal is emboldened to stand up and tell the doctor, as she exits his office, "You shouldn't keep that gargoyle in your office, it is hideous." And to remark further, "It was the first time I addressed him other than as a patient." Signaling the breakthrough, and strategic to its articulation, is this sign of horror and fear lodged in a gargoyle over which the now liberated patient has some control.

Many other examples of these narrative gearshifts—metaphors; summonings; rhetorical gestures of triumph, despair, and closure dependent on the acceptance of the associative language of dread and love that accompanies blackness—were piling up in my file. Examples I thought of as a category of sources of imagery, like water, flight, war, birth, religion, and so on, that make up the writer's kit.

These musings on Marie Cardinal's text are not in themselves wholly necessary for the book's appreciation, being simply illustrations of how each of us reads, becomes engaged in and *watches* what is being read all at the same time. I include the thoughts I had while reading this particular work because they identify the stages of my interest, first, in the pervasive use of black images and people in expressive prose; second, in the shorthand, the taken-for-granted assumptions that lie in their usage; and, finally, to the subject of this book: the sources of these images and the effect they have on the literary imagination and its product.

The principal reason these matters loom large for me is that I do not have quite the same access to these traditionally useful constructs of blackness. Neither blackness nor "people of color" stimulates in me notions of excessive, limitless love, anarchy, or routine dread. I cannot rely on these metaphorical shortcuts because I am a black writer struggling with and through a language that can powerfully evoke and enforce hidden signs of racial superiority, cultural hegemony, and dismissive "othering" of people and language which are by no means marginal or already and completely known and knowable in my work. My vulnerability would lie in romanticizing blackness rather than demonizing it; villifying whiteness rather than reifying it. The kind of work I have always wanted to do requires me to learn how to maneuver ways to free up the language from its sometimes sinister, frequently lazy, almost always predictable employment of racially informed and determined chains. (The only short story I have ever written, "Recitatif," was an experiment in the removal of all racial codes from a narrative about two characters of different races for whom racial identity is crucial.)

Writing and reading are not all that distinct for a writer. Both exercises require being alert and ready for unaccountable beauty, for the intricateness or simple elegance of the writer's imagination, for the world that imagination evokes. Both require being mindful of the places where imagination sabotages itself, locks its own gates, pollutes its vision. Writing and reading mean being aware of the writer's notions of risk and safety, the serene achievement of, or sweaty fight for, meaning and response-ability.

Antonia S. Byatt in *Possession* has described certain kinds of readings that seem to me inextricable from certain experiences of writing, "when the knowledge that we *shall know* the writing differently or better or satisfactorily runs ahead of any capacity to say what we know, or how. In these readings, a sense that the text has appeared to be wholly new, never before seen, is followed, almost immediately, by the sense that it was *always there,* that we, the readers, knew it was always there, and have *always known* it was as it was, though we have now for the first time recognised, become fully cognisant of, our knowledge."

The imagination that produces work which bears and invites rereadings, which motions to future readings as well as contemporary ones, implies a shareable world and an endlessly flexible language. Readers and writers both struggle to interpret and perform within a common language shareable imaginative worlds. And although upon that struggle the positioning of the reader has justifiable claims, the author's presence—her or his intentions, blindness, and sight—is part of the imaginative activity.

For reasons that should not need explanation here, until very recently, and regardless of the race of the author, the readers of virtually all of American fiction have been positioned as white. I am interested to know what that assumption has meant to the literary imagination. When does racial "unconsciousness" or awareness of race enrich interpretive language, and when does it impoverish it? What does positing one's writerly self, in the wholly racialized society that is the United States, as unraced and all others as raced entail? What happens to the writerly imagination of a black author who is at some level *always* conscious of representing one's own race to, or in spite of, a race of readers that understands itself to be "universal" or race-free? In other words, how is "literary whiteness" and "literary blackness" made, and what is the consequence of that construction? How do embedded assumptions of racial (not racist) language work in the literary enterprise that hopes and sometimes claims to be "humanistic"? When, in a race-conscious culture, is that lofty goal actually approximated? When not and why? Living in a nation of people who *decided* that their world view would combine agendas for individual freedom *and* mechanisms for devastating racial oppression presents a singular landscape for a writer. When this world view is taken seriously as agency, the literature produced within and without it offers an unprecedented opportunity to comprehend the resilience and gravity, the inadequacy and the force of the imaginative act.

Thinking about these matters has challenged me as a writer and a reader. It has made both activities harder and infinitely more rewarding. It has, in fact, elevated and sharpened the delight I take in the work that literature, under the pressure that racialized societies level on the creative process, manages to do. Over and over again I am amazed by the treasure trove that American literature is. How compelling is the study of those writers who take responsibility for *all* of the values they bring to their art. How stunning is the achievement of those who have searched for and mined a shareable language for the words to say it.

Toni Morrison
February 1992

contents

Playing in the Dark is the result of questions raised in three William E. Massey Sr. Lectures given at Harvard University as well as the basis of a course I teach in American literature. In an academic environment, open and demanding, I have been able to advance this inquiry and test ideas with exceptional students. The latter have been so important to this work, dedicating these pages to the classes at Princeton I have been pleased to teach is imperative. Among those students are three whose research assistance was invaluable: Dwight McBride, Pamela Ali, and especially Tara McGowan.

Major help in translating the lectures into readable manuscript came from Peter Dimock. I am grateful to him for his intelligence and his rare and graceful editorial prowess.

1
black matters

I am moved by fancies that are curled
Around these images, and cling:
The notion of some infinitely gentle
Infinitely suffering thing.

T. S. Eliot
from "Preludes, IV"

*T*hese chapters put forth an argument for extending the study of American literature into what I hope will be a wider landscape. I want to draw a map, so to speak, of a critical geography and use that map to open as much space for discovery, intellectual adventure, and close exploration as did the original charting of the New World—without the mandate for conquest. I intend to outline an attractive, fruitful, and provocative critical project, unencumbered by dreams of subversion or rallying gestures at fortress walls.

I would like it to be clear at the outset that I do not bring to these matters solely or even principally the tools of a literary critic. As a reader (before becoming a writer) I read as I had been taught to do. But books revealed themselves rather differently to me as a writer. In that capacity I have to place enormous trust in my ability to imagine others and my willingness to project consciously into the danger zones such others may represent for me. I am drawn to the ways all writers do this: the way Homer renders a heart-eating cyclops so that our hearts are wrenched with pity; the way Dostoevsky compels intimacy with Svidrigailov and Prince

Myshkin. I am in awe of the authority of Faulkner's Benjy, James's Maisie, Flaubert's Emma, Melville's Pip, Mary Shelley's Frankenstein—each of us can extend the list.

I am interested in what prompts and makes possible this process of entering what one is estranged from—and in what disables the foray, for purposes of fiction, into corners of the consciousness held off and away from the reach of the writer's imagination. My work requires me to think about how free I can be as an African-American woman writer in my genderized, sexualized, wholly racialized world. To think about (and wrestle with) the full implications of my situation leads me to consider what happens when other writers work in a highly and historically racialized society. For them, as for me, imagining is not merely looking or looking at; nor is it taking oneself intact into the other. It is, for the purposes of the work, *becoming*.

My project rises from delight, not disappointment. It rises from what I know about the ways writers transform aspects of their social grounding into aspects of language, and the ways they tell other stories, fight secret wars, limn out all sorts of debates blanketed in their text. And rises from my certainty that writers always know, at some level, that they do this.

For some time now I have been thinking about the validity or vulnerability of a certain set of assumptions conventionally accepted among literary historians and critics and circulated as "knowledge." This knowledge holds that traditional, canonical American literature is free of, uninformed, and unshaped by the four-hundred-year-old presence of, first, Africans and then African-Americans in the United States. It assumes that this presence—which shaped the body politic, the Constitution, and the entire history of the culture—has had no significant place or consequence in the origin and development of that culture's literature. Moreover, such knowledge assumes that the characteristics of our national literature emanate from a particular "Americanness" that is separate from and unaccountable to this presence. There seems to be a more or less tacit agreement among literary scholars that, because American literature has been clearly the preserve of white male views, genius, and power, those views, genius, and power are without relationship to and removed from the overwhelming presence of black people in the United States. This agreement is made about a population that preceded every American writer of renown and was, I have come to believe, one of the most furtively radical impinging forces on the country's literature. The contemplation of this black presence is central to any understanding of our national literature and should not be permitted to hover at the margins of the literary imagination.

These speculations have led me to wonder whether the major and championed characteristics of our national literature—individualism, masculinity, social engagement versus historical isolation; acute and ambiguous moral problematics; the thematics of innocence coupled with an obsession with figurations of death and hell—are not in fact responses to a dark, abiding, signing Africanist presence. It has occurred to me that the very manner by which American literature distinguishes itself as a coherent entity exists because of this unsettled and unsettling population. Just as the formation of the nation necessitated coded language and purposeful restriction to deal with the racial disingenuousness and moral frailty at its heart, so too did the literature, whose founding characteristics extend into the twentieth century, reproduce the necessity for codes and restriction. Through significant and underscored omissions, startling contradictions, heavily nuanced conflicts, through the way writers peopled their work with the signs and bodies of this presence—one can see that a real or fabricated Africanist presence was crucial to their sense of Americanness. And it shows.

.   .   .

My curiosity about the origins and literary uses of this carefully observed, and carefully invented, Africanist presence has become an informal study of what I call American Africanism. It is an investigation into the ways in which a nonwhite, Africanlike (or Africanist) presence or persona was constructed in the United States, and the imaginative uses this fabricated presence served. I am using the term "Africanism" not to suggest the larger body of knowledge on Africa that the philosopher Valentine Mudimbe means by the term "Africanism," nor to suggest the varieties and complexities of African people and their descendants who have inhabited this country. Rather I use it as a term for the denotative and connotative blackness that African peoples have come to signify, as well as the entire range of views, assumptions, readings, and misreadings that accompany Eurocentric learning about these people. As a trope, little restraint has been attached to its uses. As a disabling virus within literary discourse, Africanism has become, in the Eurocentric tradition that American education favors, both a way of talking about and a way of policing matters of class, sexual license, and repression, formations and exercises of power, and meditations on ethics and accountability. Through the simple expedient of demonizing and reifying the range of color on a palette, American Africanism makes it possible to say and not say, to inscribe and erase, to escape and engage, to act out and act on, to historicize and render timeless. It provides a way of contemplating chaos and civilization, desire and fear, and a mechanism for testing the problems and blessings of freedom.

The United States, of course, is not unique in the construction of Africanism. South America, England, France, Germany, Spain—the cultures of all these countries have participated in and contributed to some aspect of an "invented Africa." None has been able to persuade itself for long that criteria and knowledge could emerge outside the categories of domination. Among Europeans and the Europeanized, this shared process of exclusion—of assigning designation and value—has led to the popular and academic notion that racism is a "natural," if irritating, phenomenon. The literature of almost all these countries, however, is now subject to sustained critiques of its racialized discourse. The United States is a curious exception, even though it stands out as being the oldest democracy in which a black population accompanied (if one can use that word) and in many cases preceded the white settlers. Here in that nexus, with its particular formulations, and in the absence of real knowledge or open-minded inquiry about Africans and African-Americans, under the pressures of ideological and imperialistic rationales for subjugation, an American brand of Africanism emerged: strongly urged, thoroughly serviceable, companionably ego-reinforcing, and pervasive. For excellent reasons of state—because European sources of cultural hegemony were dispersed but not yet valorized in the new country—the process of organizing American coherence through a distancing Africanism became the operative mode of a new cultural hegemony.

These remarks should not be interpreted as simply an effort to move the gaze of African-American studies to a different site. I do not want to alter one hierarchy in order to institute another. It is true that I do not want to encourage those totalizing approaches to African-American scholarship which have no drive other than the exchange of dominations— dominant Eurocentric scholarship *replaced* by dominant Afrocentric scholarship. More interesting is what makes intellectual domination possible; how knowledge is transformed from invasion and conquest to revelation and choice; what ignites and informs the literary imagination, and what forces help establish the parameters of criticism.

Above all I am interested in how agendas in criticism have disguised themselves and, in so doing, impoverished the literature it studies. Criticism as a form of knowledge is capable of robbing literature not only of its own implicit and explicit ideology but of its ideas as well; it can dismiss the difficult, arduous work writers do to make an art that becomes and remains part of and significant within a human landscape. It is important to see how inextricable Africanism is or ought to be from the deliberations of literary criticism and the wanton, elaborate strategies undertaken to erase its presence from view.

What Africanism became for, and how it functioned in, the literary imagination is of paramount interest because it may be possible to discover, through a close look at literary "blackness," the nature—even the cause—of literary "whiteness." What is it *for*? What parts do the invention and development of whiteness play in the construction of what is loosely described as "American"? If such an inquiry ever comes to maturity, it may provide access to a deeper reading of American literature—a reading not completely available now, not least, I suspect, because of the studied indifference of most literary criticism to these matters.

One likely reason for the paucity of critical material on this large and compelling subject is that, in matters of race, silence and evasion have historically ruled literary discourse. Evasion has fostered another, substitute language in which the issues are encoded, foreclosing open debate. The situation is aggravated by the tremor that breaks into discourse on race. It is further complicated by the fact that the habit of ignoring race is understood to be a graceful, even generous, liberal gesture. To notice is to recognize an already discredited difference. To enforce its invisibility through silence is to allow the black body a shadowless participation in the dominant cultural body. According to this logic, every well-bred instinct argues *against noticing* and forecloses adult discourse. It is just this concept of literary and scholarly moeurs (which functions smoothly in literary criticism, but neither makes nor receives credible claims in other disciplines) that has terminated the shelf life of some once extremely well-regarded American authors and blocked access to remarkable insights in their works.

These moeurs are delicate things, however, which must be given some thought before they are abandoned. Not observing such niceties can lead to startling displays of scholarly lapses in objectivity. In 1936 an American scholar investigating the use of Negro so-called dialect in the works of Edgar Allan Poe (a short article clearly proud of its racial equanimity) opens this way: "Despite the fact that he grew up largely in the south and spent some of his most fruitful years in Richmond and Baltimore, Poe has little to say about the darky."[*]

Although I know this sentence represents the polite parlance of the day, that "darky" was understood to be a term more acceptable than "nigger," the grimace I made upon reading it was followed by an alarmed distrust of the scholar's

---

[*] Killis Campbell, "Poe's Treatment of the Negro and of the Negro Dialect," *Studies in English*, 16 (1936), p. 106.

abilities. If it seems unfair to reach back to the thirties for samples of the kind of lapse that can occur when certain manners of polite repression are waived, let me assure you equally egregious representations of the phenomenon are still common.

Another reason for this quite ornamental vacuum in literary discourse on the presence and influence of Africanist peoples in American criticism is the pattern of thinking about racialism in terms of its consequences on the victim—of always defining it assymetrically from the perspective of its impact on the object of racist policy and attitudes. A good deal of time and intelligence has been invested in the exposure of racism and the horrific results on its objects. There are constant, if erratic, liberalizing efforts to legislate these matters. There are also powerful and persuasive attempts to analyze the origin and fabrication of racism itself, contesting the assumption that it is an inevitable, permanent, and eternal part of all social landscapes. I do not wish to disparage these inquiries. It is precisely because of them that any progress at all has been accomplished in matters of racial discourse. But that well-established study should be joined with another, equally important one: the impact of racism on those who perpetuate it. It seems both poignant and striking how avoided and unanalyzed is the effect of racist inflection on the subject. What I propose here is to examine the impact of notions of racial hierarchy, racial exclusion, and racial vulnerability and availability on nonblacks who held, resisted, explored, or altered those notions. The scholarship that looks into the mind, imagination, and behavior of slaves is valuable. But equally valuable is a serious intellectual effort to see what racial ideology does to the mind, imagination, and behavior of masters.

Historians have approached these areas, as have social scientists, anthropologists, psychiatrists, and some students of comparative literature. Literary scholars have begun to pose these questions of various national literatures. Urgently needed is the same kind of attention paid to the literature of the western country that has one of the most resilient Africanist populations in the world—a population that has always had a curiously intimate and unhingingly separate existence within the dominant one. When matters of race are located and called attention to in American literature, critical response has tended to be on the order of a humanistic nostrum—or a dismissal mandated by the label "political." Excising the political from the life of the mind is a sacrifice that has proven costly. I think of this erasure as a kind of trembling hypochondria always curing itself with unnecessary surgery. A criticism that needs to insist that literature is not only "universal" but also "race-free" risks lobotomizing that literature, and diminishes both the art and the artist.

I am vulnerable to the inference here that my inquiry has vested interests; that because I am an African-American and a writer I stand to benefit in ways not limited to intellectual fulfillment from this line of questioning. I will have to risk the accusation because the point is too important: for both black and white American writers, in a wholly racialized society, there is no escape from racially inflected language, and the work writers do to unhobble the imagination from the demands of that language is complicated, interesting, and definitive.

Like thousands of avid but nonacademic readers, some powerful literary critics in the United States have never read, and are proud to say so, *any* African-American text. It seems to have done them no harm, presented them with no discernible limitations in the scope of their work or influence. I suspect, with much evidence to support the suspicion, that they will continue to flourish without any knowledge whatsoever of African-American literature. What is fascinating, however, is to observe how their lavish exploration of literature manages *not* to see meaning in the thunderous, theatrical presence of black surrogacy—an informing, stabilizing, and disturbing element—in the literature they do study. It is interesting, not surprising, that the arbiters of critical power in American literature seem to take pleasure in, indeed relish, their ignorance of African-American texts. What is surprising is that their refusal to read black texts—a refusal that makes no disturbance in their intellectual life—repeats itself when they reread the traditional, established works of literature worthy of their attention.

It is possible, for example, to read Henry James scholarship exhaustively and never arrive at a nodding mention, much less a satisfactory treatment, of the black woman who lubricates the turn of the plot and becomes the agency of moral choice and meaning in *What Maisie Knew*. Never are we invited to a reading of "The Beast in the Jungle" in which that figuration is followed to what seems to me its logical conclusion. It is hard to think of any aspect of Gertrude Stein's *Three Lives* that has not been covered, except the exploratory and explanatory uses to which she puts the black woman who holds center stage in that work. The urgency and anxiety in Willa Cather's rendering of black characters are liable to be missed entirely; no mention is made of the problem that race causes in the technique and the credibility of her last novel, *Sapphira and the Slave Girl*. These critics see no excitement or meaning in the tropes of darkness, sexuality, and desire in Ernest Hemingway or in his cast of black men. They see no connection between God's grace and Africanist "othering" in Flannery O'Connor. With few exceptions, Faulkner criticism collapses the major themes of that writer into discursive "mythologies" and treats the later works—whose focus is race and class—as minor, superficial, marked by decline.

An instructive parallel to this willed scholarly indifference is the centuries-long, hysterical blindness to feminist discourse and the way in which women and women's issues were read (or unread). Blatant sexist readings are on the decline, and where they still exist they have little effect because of the successful appropriation by women of their own discourse.

National literatures, like writers, get along the best way they can, and with what they can. Yet they do seem to end up describing and inscribing what is really on the national mind. For the most part, the literature of the United States has taken as its concern the architecture of a *new white man*. If I am disenchanted by the indifference of literary criticism toward examining the range of that concern, I do have a lasting resort: the writers themselves.

Writers are among the most sensitive, the most intellectually anarchic, most representative, most probing of artists. The ability of writers to imagine what is not the self, to familiarize the strange and mystify the familiar, is the test of their power. The languages they use and the social and historical context in which these languages signify are indirect and direct revelations of that power and its limitations. So it is to them, the creators of American literature, that I look for clarification about the invention and effect of Africanism in the United States.

My early assumptions as a reader were that black people signified little or nothing in the imagination of white American writers. Other than as the objects of an occasional bout of jungle fever, other than to provide local color or to lend some touch of verisimilitude or to supply a needed moral gesture, humor, or bit of pathos, blacks made no appearance at all. This was a reflection, I thought, of the marginal impact that blacks had on the lives of the characters in the work as well as the creative imagination of the author. To imagine or write otherwise, to situate black people throughout the pages and scenes of a book like some government quota, would be ludicrous and dishonest.

But then I stopped reading as a reader and began to read as a writer. Living in a racially articulated and predicated world, I could not be alone in reacting to this aspect of the American cultural and historical condition. I began to see how the literature I revered, the literature I loathed, behaved in its encounter with racial ideology. American literature could not help being shaped by that encounter. Yes, I wanted to identify those moments when American literature was complicit in the fabrication of racism, but equally important, I wanted to see when literature exploded and undermined it. Still, those were minor concerns. Much more important was to contemplate how Africanist personae, narrative, and idiom moved and enriched the text in self-conscious ways, to consider what the engagement meant for the work of the writer's imagination.

How does literary utterance arrange itself when it tries to imagine an Africanist other? What are the signs, the codes, the literary strategies designed to accommodate this encounter? What does the inclusion of Africans or African-Americans do to and for the work? As a reader my assumption had always been that nothing "happens": Africans and their descendants were not, in any sense that matters, *there;* and when they were there, they were decorative—displays of the agile writer's technical expertise. I assumed that since the author was not black, the appearance of Africanist characters or narrative or idiom in a work could never be *about* anything other than the "normal," unracialized, illusory white world that provided the fictional backdrop. Certainly no American text of the sort I am discussing was ever written *for* black people—no more than *Uncle Tom's Cabin* was written for

Uncle Tom to read or be persuaded by. As a writer reading, I came to realize the obvious: the subject of the dream is the dreamer. The fabrication of an Africanist persona is reflexive; an extraordinary meditation on the self; a powerful exploration of the fears and desires that reside in the writerly conscious. It is an astonishing revelation of longing, of terror, of perplexity, of shame, of magnanimity. It requires hard work *not* to see this.

It is as if I had been looking at a fishbowl—the glide and flick of the golden scales, the green tip, the bolt of white careening back from the gills; the castles at the bottom, surrounded by pebbles and tiny, intricate fronds of green; the barely disturbed water, the flecks of waste and food, the tranquil bubbles traveling to the surface—and suddenly I saw the bowl, the structure that transparently (and invisibly) permits the ordered life it contains to exist in the larger world. In other words, I began to rely on my knowledge of how books get written, how language arrives; my sense of how and why writers abandon or take on certain aspects of their project. I began to rely on my understanding of what the linguistic struggle requires of writers and what they make of the surprise that is the inevitable concomitant of the act of creation. What became transparent were the self-evident ways that Americans choose to talk about themselves through and within a sometimes allegorical, sometimes metaphorical, but always choked representation of an Africanist presence.

·   ·   ·

I have made much here of a kind of willful critical blindness—
a blindness that, if it had not existed, could have made these
insights part of our routine literary heritage. Habit, manners,
and political agenda have contributed to this refusal of critical
insight. A case in point is Willa Cather's *Sapphira and the
Slave Girl,* a text that has been virtually jettisoned from the
body of American literature by critical consensus.

References to this novel in much Cather scholarship are
apologetic, dismissive, even cutting in their brief documenta-
tion of its flaws—of which there are a sufficient number.
What remains less acknowledged is the source of its flaws and
the conceptual problems that the book both poses and represents. Simply to assert the failure of Cather's gifts, the exhaustion of her perception, the narrowing of her canvas, evades
the obligation to look carefully at what might have caused
the book to fail—if "failure" is an intelligent term to apply
to any fiction. (It is as if the realms of fiction and reality
were divided by a line that, when maintained, offers the possibility of winning but, when crossed, signals the inevitability
of losing.)

I suspect that the "problem" of *Sapphira and the Slave
Girl* is not that it has a weaker vision or is the work of a
weaker mind. The problem is trying to come to terms criti-
cally and artistically with the novel's concerns: the power and
license of a white slave mistress over her female slaves. How
can that *content* be subsumed by some other meaning? How
can the story of a white mistress be severed from a consider-
ation of race and the violence entailed in the story's premise?

If *Sapphira and the Slave Girl* neither pleases nor engages us, it may be enlightening to discover why. It is as if this last book—this troublesome, quietly dismissed novel, very important to Cather—is not only about a fugitive but is itself a fugitive from its author's literary estate. It is also a book that describes and inscribes its narrative's own fugitive flight from itself.

Our first hint of this flight appears in the title, *Sapphira and the Slave Girl*. The girl referred to is named Nancy. To have called the book "Sapphira and Nancy" would have lured Cather into dangerous deep water. Such a title would have clarified and drawn attention immediately to what the novel obscures even as it makes a valiant effort at honest engagement: the sycophancy of white identity. The story, briefly, is this.

Sapphira Colbert, an invalid confined to her chair and dependent on slaves for the most intimate services, has persuaded herself that her husband is having or aching to have a liaison with Nancy, the pubescent daughter of her most devoted female slave. It is clear from the beginning that Mistress Colbert is in error: Nancy is pure to the point of vapidity; Master Colbert is a man of modest habits, ambition, and imagination.

Sapphira's suspicions, fed by her feverish imagination and by her leisure to have them, grow and luxuriate unbearably. She forms a plan. She will invite a malleable lecherous nephew, Martin, to visit and let his nature run its course: Nancy will be seduced. The purpose of arranging the rape of her young servant is to reclaim, for purposes not made clear, the full attentions of her husband.

Interference with these plans comes from Sapphira's daughter, Rachel, estranged from her mother primarily for her abolitionist views but also, we are led to believe, because Sapphira does not tolerate opposition. It is Rachel who manages to effect Nancy's escape to the north and freedom, with the timid help of her father, Mr. Colbert. A reconciliation of all of the white characters takes place when the daughter loses one of her children to diphtheria and is blessed with the recuperation of the other. The reconciliation of the two key black characters is rendered in a postscript in which many years later Nancy returns to see her aged mother and recount her post-flight adult narrative to the author, a child witnessing the return and the happiness that is the novel's denouement. The novel was published in 1940, but has the shape and feel of a tale written or experienced much earlier.

This précis in no way does justice to the novel's complexities and its problems of execution. Both arise, I believe, not because Cather was failing in narrative power, but because of her struggle to address an almost completely buried subject: the interdependent working of power, race, and sexuality in a white woman's battle for coherence.

In some ways this novel is a classic fugitive slave narrative: a thrilling escape to freedom. But we learn almost nothing of the trials of the fugitive's journey because the emphasis is on Nancy's fugitive state within the household *before her escape*. And the real fugitive, the text asserts, is the slave mistress. Furthermore, the plot escapes the author's control and, as its own fugitive status becomes clear, is destined to point to the hopelessness of excising racial considerations from formulations of white identity.

Escape is the central focus of Nancy's existence on the Colbert farm. From the moment of her first appearance, she is forced to hide her emotions, her thoughts, and eventually her body from pursuers. Unable to please Sapphira, plagued by the jealousy of the darker-skinned slaves, she is also barred from help, instruction, or consolation from her own mother, Till. That condition could only prevail in a slave society where the mistress can count on (and an author can believe the reader does not object to) the complicity of a mother in the seduction and rape of her own daughter. Because Till's loyalty to and responsibility for her mistress is so primary, it never occurs and need not occur to Sapphira that Till might be hurt or alarmed by the violence planned for her only child. That assumption is based on another—that slave women are not mothers; they are "natally dead," with no obligations to their offspring or their own parents.

This breach startles the contemporary reader and renders Till an unbelievable and unsympathetic character. It is a problem that Cather herself seems hard put to address. She both acknowledges and banishes this wholly unanalyzed mother-daughter relationship by inserting a furtive exchange between Till and Rachel in chapter 10:

> ". . . Till asked in a low, cautious murmur: 'You ain't heard nothin', Miss Rachel?'

'Not yet. When I do hear, I'll let you know. I saw her into good hands, Till. I don't doubt she's in Canada by this time, amongst English people.'

'Thank you, mam, Miss Rachel. I can't say no more. I don't want them niggers to see me cryin'. If she's up there with the English folks, she'll have some chance.'" *

The passage seems to come out of nowhere because there has been nothing in a hundred or so pages to prepare us for such maternal concern. "You ain't heard nothin'?" Till asks of Rachel. Just that—those four words—meaning: Is Nancy all right? Did she arrive safely? Is she alive? Is anybody after her? All of these questions lie in the one she does manage to ask.

Surrounding this dialogue is the silence of four hundred years. It leaps out of the novel's void and out of the void of historical discourse on slave parent-child relationships and pain. The contemporary reader is relieved when Till finally finds the language and occasion to make this inquiry about the fate of her daughter. But nothing more is made of it. And the reader is asked to believe that the silence surrounding the inquiry as well as its delay are due to Till's greater concern about her status among dark-skinned "field" niggers. Clearly Cather was driven to create the exchange not to rehabilitate Till in our readerly eyes but because at some point the silence

---

*Willa Cather, *Sapphira and the Slave Girl* (New York: Alfred A. Knopf, 1940), p. 249.

became an unbearable violence, even in a work full of violence and evasion. Consider the pressures exerted by the subject: the need to portray the faithful slave; the compelling attraction of exploring the possibilities of one woman's absolute power over the body of another woman; confrontation with an uncontested assumption of the sexual availability of black females; the need to make credible the bottomless devotion of the person on whom Sapphira is totally dependent. It is after all *hers,* this slave woman's body, in a way that her own invalid flesh is not. These fictional demands stretch to breaking all narrative coherence. It is no wonder that Nancy cannot think up her own escape and must be urged into taking the risk.

Nancy has to hide her interior life from hostile fellow slaves *and* her own mother. The absence of camaraderie between Nancy and the other slave women turns on the device of color fetish—the skin-color privilege that Nancy enjoys because she is lighter than the others and therefore enviable. The absence of mother love, always a troubling concern of Cather's, is connected to the assumption of a slave's natal isolation. These are bizarre and disturbing deformations of reality that normally lie mute in novels containing Africanist characters, but Cather does not repress them altogether. The character she creates is at once a fugitive within the household and a sign of the sterility of the fiction-making imagination when there is no available language to clarify or even name the source of unbelievability.

Interestingly, the other major cause of Nancy's constant state of flight is wholly credible: that she should be unarmed in the face of the nephew's sexual assault and that she alone is responsible for extracting herself from the crisis. We do not question her vulnerability. What becomes titillating in this wicked pursuit of innocence—what makes it something other than an American variant of *Clarissa*—is the racial component. The nephew is not even required to court or flatter Nancy. After an unsuccessful reach for her from the branches of a cherry tree, he can, and plans to, simply arrive wherever she is sleeping. And since Sapphira has ordered her to sleep in the hall on a pallet, Nancy is forced to sneak away in the dark to quarters where she may be, but is not certain to be, safe. Other than Rachel, the pro-abolitionist, Nancy has access to no one to whom she can complain, explain, object, or from whom she can seek protection. We must accept her total lack of initiative, for there are no exits. She has no recourse—except in miserable looks that arouse Rachel's curiosity.

Nor is there any law, if the nephew succeeds in the rape, to entertain her complaint. If she becomes pregnant as a result of the violence, the issue is a boon to the economy of the estate, not an injury to it. There is no father or, in this case, "stepfather" to voice a protest on Nancy's behalf, since honor was the first thing stripped from the man. He is a "capon," we are told, given to Till so that she will have no more children and can give her full attention and energy to Mistress Sapphira.

Rendered voiceless, a cipher, a perfect victim, Nancy runs the risk of losing the reader's interest. In a curious way,

Sapphira's plotting, like Cather's plot, is without reference to the characters and exists solely for the ego-gratification of the slave mistress. This becomes obvious when we consider what would have been the consequences of a successful rape. Given the novel's own terms, there can be no grounds for Sapphira's thinking that Nancy can be "ruined" in the conventional sense. There is no question of marriage to Martin, to Colbert, to anybody. Then, too, why would such an assault move her slave girl outside her husband's interest? The probability is that it would secure it. If Mr. Colbert is tempted by Nancy the chaste, is there anything in slavocracy to make him disdain Nancy the unchaste?

Such a breakdown in the logic and machinery of plot construction implies the powerful impact race has on narrative—and on narrative strategy. Nancy is not only the victim of Sapphira's evil, whimsical scheming. She becomes the unconsulted, appropriated ground of Cather's inquiry into what is of paramount importance to the author: the reckless, unabated power of a white woman gathering identity unto herself from the wholly available and serviceable lives of Africanist others. This seems to me to provide the coordinates of an immensely important moral debate.

This novel is not a story of a mean, vindictive mistress; it is the story of a desperate one. It concerns a troubled, disappointed woman confined to the prison of her defeated flesh, whose social pedestal rests on the sturdy spine of racial degradation; whose privileged gender has nothing that elevates it except color, and whose moral posture collapses without a whimper before the greater necessity of self-esteem, even though the source of that esteem is a delusion. For Sapphira too is a fugitive in this novel, committed to escape: from the possibility of developing her own adult personality and her own sensibilities; from her femaleness; from motherhood; from the community of women; from her body.

She escapes the necessity of inhabiting her own body by dwelling on the young, healthy, and sexually appetizing Nancy. She has transferred its care into the hands of others. In this way she escapes her illness, decay, confinement, anonymity, and physical powerlessness. In other words, she has the leisure and the instruments to construct a self; but the self she constructs must be—is conceivable only as—white. The surrogate black bodies become her hands and feet, her fantasies of sexual ravish and intimacy with her husband, and, not inconsiderably, her sole source of love.

If the Africanist characters and their condition are removed from the text of *Sapphira and the Slave Girl* we will not have a Miss Havisham immured or in flames. We have nothing: no process of deranged self-construction that can take for granted acquiescence in so awful an enterprise; no drama of limitless power. Sapphira can hide far more successfully than Nancy. She can, and does, remain outside the normal requirements of adult womanhood because of the infantilized Africanist population at her disposal.

The final fugitive in Cather's novel is the novel itself. The plot's own plotting to free the endangered slave girl (of no apparent interest, as we have seen, to the girl's mother or her slave associates) is designed for quite other purposes. It functions as a means for the author to meditate on the moral equivalence of free white women and enslaved black women. The fact that these equations are designed as mother-daughter pairings and relationships leads to the inescapable conclusion that Cather was dreaming and redreaming her problematic relationship with her own mother.

The imaginative strategy is a difficult one at best, an impossible one in the event—so impossible that Cather permits the novel to escape from the pages of fiction into nonfiction. For narrative credibility she substitutes her own determination to force the equation. It is an equation that must take place outside the narrative.

Sapphira and the Slave Girl turns at the end into a kind of memoir, the author's recollection of herself as a child witnessing the return, the reconciliation, and an imposed "all rightness" in untenable, outrageous circumstances. The silenced, acquiescent Africanist characters in the narrative are not less muzzled in the epilogue. The reunion—the drama of it, like its narrative function—is no more the slave characters' than their slave lives have been. The reunion is literally stage-managed for the author, now become a child. Till agrees to wait until little Willa is at the doorway before she permits herself the first sight she has had of her daughter in twenty-five years.

Only with Africanist characters is such a project thinkable: delayed gratification for the pleasure of a (white) child. When the embrace is over, Willa the white child accompanies the black mother and daughter into their narrative, listening to the dialogue but intervening in it at every turn. The shape and detail and substance of their lives are hers, not theirs. Just as Sapphira has employed these surrogate, serviceable black bodies for her own purposes of power without risk, so the author employs them in behalf of her own desire for a *safe* participation in loss, in love, in chaos, in justice.

But things go awry. As often happens, characters make claims, impose demands of imaginative accountability over and above the author's will to contain them. Just as Rachel's intervention foils Sapphira's plot, so Cather's urgent need to know and understand this Africanist mother and daughter requires her to give them center stage. The child Cather listens to Till's stories, and the slave, silenced in the narrative, has the final words of the epilogue.

Yet even, or especially, here where the novel ends Cather feels obliged to gesture compassionately toward slavery. Through Till's agency the elevating benevolence of the institution is invoked. Serviceable to the last, this Africanist presence is permitted speech only to reinforce the slaveholders' ideology, in spite of the fact that it subverts the entire premise of the novel. Till's voluntary genuflection is as ecstatic as it is suspicious.

In returning to her childhood, at the end of her writing career, Cather returns to a very personal, indeed private experience. In her last novel she works out and toward the meaning of female betrayal as it faces the void of racism. She may not have arrived safely, like Nancy, but to her credit she did undertake the dangerous journey.

2
romancing the shadow

. . . shadows
Bigger than people and blacker than niggers . . .

Robert Penn Warren
from "Penological Studies: Southern Exposure, 3"

$\mathcal{A}$t the end of *The Narrative of Arthur Gordon Pym*, Edgar Allan Poe describes the last two days of an extraordinary journey:

"*March 21st.*—A sullen darkness now hovered above us—but from out the milky depths of the ocean a luminous glare arose, and stole up along the bulwarks of the boat. We were nearly overwhelmed by the white ashy shower which settled upon us and upon the canoe, but melted into the water as it fell . . .

"*March 22d.*—The darkness had materially increased, relieved only by the glare of the water thrown back from the white curtain before us. Many gigantic and pallidly white birds flew continuously now from beyond the veil, and their scream was the eternal *Tekeli-li!* as they retreated from our vision. Hereupon Nu-Nu stirred in the bottom of the boat; but upon touching him, we found his spirit departed. And now we rushed into the embraces of the cataract, where a chasm threw itself open to receive us. But there arose in our pathway a shrouded human figure, very far larger in its proportions than any dweller among men. And the hue of the skin of the figure was of the perfect whiteness of the snow."

They have been floating, Pym and Peters and the native, Nu-Nu, on a warm, milk-white sea under a "white ashy shower." The black man dies, and the boat rushes on through the white curtain behind which a white giant rises up. After that, there is nothing. There is no more narrative. Instead there is a scholarly note, explanation, and an anxious, piled-up "conclusion." The latter states that it was *whiteness* that terrified the natives and killed Nu-Nu. The following inscription was carved into the walls of the chasms the travelers passed through: "I have graven it in within the hills, and my vengeance upon the dust within the rock."

No early American writer is more important to the concept of American Africanism than Poe. And no image is more telling than the one just described: the visualized but somehow closed and unknowable white form that rises from the mists at the end of the journey—or, at any rate, at the end of the narration proper. The images of the white curtain and the "shrouded human figure" with skin "the perfect whiteness of the snow" both occur after the narrative has encountered blackness. The first white image seems related to the expiration and erasure of the serviceable and serving black figure, Nu-Nu. Both are figurations of impenetrable whiteness that surface in American literature whenever an

Africanist presence is engaged. These closed white images are found frequently, but not always, at the end of the narrative. They appear so often and in such particular circumstances that they give pause. They clamor, it seems, for an attention that would yield the meaning that lies in their positioning, their repetition, and their strong suggestion of paralysis and incoherence; of impasse and non-sequitur.

These images of impenetrable whiteness need contextualizing to explain their extraordinary power, pattern, and consistency. Because they appear almost always in conjunction with representations of black or Africanist people who are dead, impotent, or under complete control, these images of blinding whiteness seem to function as both antidote for and meditation on the shadow that is companion to this whiteness—a dark and abiding presence that moves the hearts and texts of American literature with fear and longing. This haunting, a darkness from which our early literature seemed unable to extricate itself, suggests the complex and contradictory situation in which American writers found themselves during the formative years of the nation's literature.

Young America distinguished itself by, and understood itself to be, pressing toward a future of freedom, a kind of human dignity believed unprecedented in the world. A whole tradition of "universal" yearnings collapsed into that well-fondled phrase, "the American Dream." Although this immigrant dream deserves the exhaustive scrutiny it has received in the scholarly disciplines and the arts, it is just as important to know what these people were rushing from as it is to know what they were hastening to. If the New World fed dreams, what was the Old World reality that whetted the appetite for them? And how did that reality caress and grip the shaping of a new one?

The flight from the Old World to the New is generally seen to be a flight from oppression and limitation to freedom and possibility. Although, in fact, the escape was sometimes an escape from license—from a society perceived to be unacceptably permissive, ungodly, and undisciplined—for those fleeing for reasons other than religious ones, constraint and limitation impelled the journey. All the Old World offered these immigrants was poverty, prison, social ostracism, and, not infrequently, death. There was of course a clerical, scholarly group of immigrants who came seeking the adventure possible in founding a colony for, rather than against, one or another mother country or fatherland. And of course there were the merchants, who came for the cash.

Whatever the reasons, the attraction was of the "clean slate" variety, a once-in-a-lifetime opportunity not only to be born again but to be born again in new clothes, as it were. The new setting would provide new raiments of self. This second chance could even benefit from the mistakes of the first. In the New World there was the vision of a limitless future, made more gleaming by the constraint, dissatisfaction, and turmoil left behind. It was a promise genuinely promising. With luck and endurance one could discover freedom; find a way to make God's law manifest; or end up rich as a prince. The desire for freedom is preceded by oppression;

a yearning for God's law is born of the detestation of human license and corruption; the glamor of riches is in thrall to poverty, hunger, and debt.

There was very much more in the late seventeenth and eighteenth centuries to make the trip worth the risk. The habit of genuflection would be replaced by the thrill of command. Power—control of one's own destiny—would replace the powerlessness felt before the gates of class, caste, and cunning persecution. One could move from discipline and punishment to disciplining and punishing; from social ostracism to social rank. One could be released from a useless, binding, repulsive past into a kind of history-lessness, a blank page waiting to be inscribed. Much was to be written there: noble impulses were made into law and appropriated for a national tradition; base ones, learned and elaborated in the rejected and rejecting homeland, were also made into law and appropriated for tradition.

The body of literature produced by the young nation is one way it inscribed its transactions with these fears, forces, and hopes. And it is difficult to read the literature of young America without being struck by how antithetical it is to our modern rendition of the American Dream. How pronounced in it is the absence of that term's elusive mixture of hope, realism, materialism, and promise. For a people who made much of their "newness"—their potential, freedom, and innocence—it is striking how dour, how troubled, how frightened and haunted our early and founding literature truly is.

We have words and labels for this haunting—"gothic," "romantic," "sermonic," "Puritan"—whose sources are to be found in the literature of the world these immigrants left. But the strong affinity between the nineteenth-century American psyche and gothic romance has rightly been much remarked. Why should a young country repelled by Europe's moral and social disorder, swooning in a fit of desire and rejection, devote its talents to reproducing in its own literature the typology of diabolism it wanted to leave behind? An answer to that seems fairly obvious: one way to benefit from the lessons of earlier mistakes and past misfortune is to record them so as to prevent their repetition through exposure and inoculation.

Romance was the form in which this uniquely American prophylaxis could be played out. Long after the movement in Europe, romance remained the cherished expression of young America. What was there in American romanticism that made it so attractive to Americans as a battle plain on which to fight, engage, and imagine their demons?

It has been suggested that romance is an evasion of history (and thus perhaps attractive to a people trying to evade the recent past). But I am more persuaded by arguments that find in it the head-on encounter with very real, pressing historical forces and the contradictions inherent in them as they came to be experienced by writers. Romance, an exploration of anxiety imported from the shadows of European culture, made possible the sometimes safe and other times risky embrace of quite specific, understandably human, fears:

Americans' fear of being outcast, of failing, of powerlessness; their fear of boundarylessness, of Nature unbridled and crouched for attack; their fear of the absence of so-called civilization; their fear of loneliness, of aggression both external and internal. In short, the terror of human freedom—the thing they coveted most of all. Romance offered writers not less but more; not a narrow a-historical canvas but a wide historical one; not escape but entanglement. For young America it had everything: nature as subject matter, a system of symbolism, a thematics of the search for self-valorization and validation—above all, the opportunity to conquer fear imaginatively and to quiet deep insecurities. It offered platforms for moralizing and fabulation, and for the imaginative entertainment of violence, sublime incredibility, and terror—and terror's most significant, overweening ingredient: darkness, with all the connotative value it awakened.

There is no romance free of what Herman Melville called "the power of blackness," especially not in a country in which there was a resident population, already black, upon which the imagination could play; through which historical, moral, metaphysical, and social fears, problems, and dichotomies could be articulated. The slave population, it could be and was assumed, offered itself up as surrogate selves for meditation on problems of human freedom, its lure and its elusiveness. This black population was available for meditations on terror—the terror of European outcasts, their dread of failure, powerlessness, Nature without limits, natal loneliness, internal aggression, evil, sin, greed. In other words, this slave population was understood to have offered itself up for reflections on human freedom in terms other than the abstractions of human potential and the rights of man.

The ways in which artists—and the society that bred them—transferred internal conflicts to a "blank darkness," to conveniently bound and violently silenced black bodies, is a major theme in American literature. The rights of man, for example, an organizing principle upon which the nation was founded, was inevitably yoked to Africanism. Its history, its origin is permanently allied with another seductive concept: the hierarchy of race. As the sociologist Orlando Patterson has noted, we should not be surprised that the Enlightenment could accommodate slavery; we should be surprised if it had not. The concept of freedom did not emerge in a vacuum. Nothing highlighted freedom—if it did not in fact create it—like slavery.

Black slavery enriched the country's creative possibilities. For in that construction of blackness *and* enslavement could be found not only the not-free but also, with the dramatic polarity created by skin color, the projection of the not-me. The result was a playground for the imagination. What rose up out of collective needs to allay internal fears and to rationalize external exploitation was an American Africanism—a fabricated brew of darkness, otherness, alarm, and desire that is uniquely American. (There also exists, of course, a European Africanism with a counterpart in colonial literature.)

What I wish to examine is how the image of reined-in,

bound, suppressed, and repressed darkness became objectified in American literature as an Africanist persona. I want to show how the duties of that persona—duties of exorcism and reification and mirroring—are on demand and on display throughout much of the literature of the country and helped to form the distinguishing characteristics of a proto-American literature.

Earlier I said that cultural identities are formed and informed by a nation's literature, and that what seemed to be on the "mind" of the literature of the United States was the self-conscious but highly problematic construction of the American as a new white man. Emerson's call for that new man in "The American Scholar" indicates the deliberateness of the construction, the conscious necessity for establishing difference. But the writers who responded to this call, accepting or rejecting it, did not look solely to Europe to establish a reference for difference. There was a very theatrical difference underfoot. Writers were able to celebrate or deplore an identity already existing or rapidly taking a form that was elaborated through racial difference. That difference provided a huge payout of sign, symbol, and agency in the process of organizing, separating, and consolidating identity along culturally valuable lines of interest.

Bernard Bailyn has provided us with an extraordinary investigation of European settlers in the act of becoming Americans. I want to quote a rather long passage from his *Voyagers to the West* because it underscores the salient aspects of the American character I have been describing:

"William Dunbar, seen through his letters and diary, appears to be more fictional than real—a creature of William Faulkner's imagination, a more cultivated Colonel Sutpen but no less mysterious. He too, like that strange character in *Absalom! Absalom!*, was a man in his early twenties who appeared suddenly in the Mississippi wilderness to stake out a claim to a large parcel of land, then disappeared to the Caribbean, to return leading a battalion of 'wild' slaves with whose labor alone he built an estate where before there had been nothing but trees and uncultivated soil. But he was more complex than Sutpen, if no less driving in his early ambitions, no less a progenitor of a notable southern family, and no less a part of a violent biracial world whose tensions could lead in strange directions. For this wilderness planter was a scientist, who would later correspond with Jefferson on science and exploration, a Mississippi planter whose contributions to the American Philosophical Society (to which Jefferson proposed him for membership) included linguistics, archaeology, hydrostatics, astronomy, and climatology, and whose geographical explorations were reported in widely known publications. Like Sutpen an exotic figure in the plantation world of early Mississippi—known as 'Sir' William just as Sutpen was known as 'Colonel'— he too imported into that raw, half-savage world the niceties of European culture: not chandeliers and costly rugs, but books, surveyor's equipment of the finest kind, and the latest instruments of science.

"Dunbar was a Scot by birth, the youngest son of Sir Archibald Dunbar of Morayshire. He was educated first by tutors at home, then at the university in Aberdeen, where his interest in mathematics, astronomy, and belles-lettres took mature shape. What happened to him after his return home and later in London, where he circulated with young intellectuals, what propelled, or led, him out of the metropolis on the first leg of his long voyage west is not known. But whatever his motivation may have been, in April 1771, aged only twenty-two, Dunbar appeared in Philadelphia . . .

"Ever eager for gentility, this well-educated product of the Scottish enlightenment and of London's sophistication—this bookish young *littérateur* and scientist who, only five years earlier, had been corresponding about scientific problems—about 'Dean Swifts beatitudes,' about the 'virtuous and happy life,' and about the Lord's commandment that mankind should 'love one another'—was yet strangely insensitive to the suffering of those who served him. In July 1776 he recorded not the independence of the American colonies from Britain, but the suppression of an alleged conspiracy for freedom by slaves on his own plantation . . .

"Dunbar, the young *érudit,* the Scottish scientist

and man of letters, was no sadist. His plantation regime was, by the standards of the time, mild; he clothed and fed his slaves decently, and frequently relented in his more severe punishments. But 4,000 miles from the sources of culture, alone on the far periphery of British civilization where physical survival was a daily struggle, where ruthless exploitation was a way of life, and where disorder, violence, and human degradation were commonplace, he had triumphed by successful adaptation. Endlessly enterprising and resourceful, his finer sensibilities dulled by the abrasions of frontier life, and feeling within himself a sense of authority and autonomy he had not known before, a force that flowed from his absolute control over the lives of others, he emerged a distinctive new man, a borderland gentleman, a man of property in a raw, half-savage world."*

Let me call attention to some elements of this portrait, some pairings and interdependencies that are marked in the story of William Dunbar. First there is the historical connection between the Enlightenment and the institution of slavery—the rights of man and his enslavement. Second, we have the relationship between Dunbar's education and his New World enterprise. The education he had was exceptional

---

*Bernard Bailyn, *Voyagers to the West: A Passage in the Peopling of America on the Eve of the Revolution* (New York: Alfred A. Knopf, 1986), pp. 488–492.

and exceptionally cultivated: it included the latest thought on theology and science, an effort perhaps to make them mutually accountable, to make one support the other. He is not only a "product of the Scottish enlightenment" but a London intellectual as well. He read Jonathan Swift, discussed the Christian commandment to love one another, and is described as "strangely" insensitive to the suffering of his slaves. On July 12, 1776, he records with astonishment and hurt surprise a slave rebellion on his plantation: "Judge my surprise . . . Of what avail is kindness & good usage when rewarded by such ingratitude." "Constantly bewildered," Bailyn goes on, "by his slaves' behavior . . . [Dunbar] recovered two runaways and 'condemned them to receive 500 lashes each at five different times, and to carry a chain & log fixt to the ancle.'"

I take this to be a succinct portrait of the process by which the American as new, white, and male was constituted. It is a formation with at least four desirable consequences, all of which are referred to in Bailyn's summation of Dunbar's character and located in how Dunbar felt "within himself." Let me repeat: "a sense of authority and autonomy he had not known before, a force that flowed from his absolute control over the lives of others, he emerged a distinctive new man, a borderland gentleman, a man of property in a raw, half-savage world." A power, a sense of freedom, he had not known before. But what had he known before? Fine education, London sophistication, theological and scientific thought. None of these, one gathers, could provide him with the authority and autonomy that Mississippi planter life did. Also this sense is understood to be a force that flows, already present and ready to spill as a result of his "absolute control over the lives of others." This force is not a willed domination, a thought-out, calculated choice, but rather a kind of natural resource, a Niagara Falls waiting to drench Dunbar as soon as he is in a position to assume absolute control. Once he has moved into that position, he is resurrected as a new man, a distinctive man—a different man. And whatever his social status in London, in the New World he is a gentleman. More gentle, more man. The site of his transformation is within rawness: he is backgrounded by savagery.

·   ·   ·

I want to suggest that these concerns—autonomy, authority, newness and difference, absolute power—not only become the major themes and presumptions of American literature, but that each one is made possible by, shaped by, activated by a complex awareness and employment of a constituted Africanism. It was this Africanism, deployed as rawness and savagery, that provided the staging ground and arena for the elaboration of the quintessential American identity.

Autonomy is freedom and translates into the much championed and revered "individualism"; newness translates into "innocence"; distinctiveness becomes difference and the erection of strategies for maintaining it; authority and absolute power become a romantic, conquering "heroism," virility, and the problematics of wielding absolute power over the lives of others. All the rest are made possible by this last, it would seem—absolute power called forth and played against and within a natural and mental landscape conceived of as a "raw, half-savage world."

Why is it seen as raw and savage? Because it is peopled by a nonwhite indigenous population? Perhaps. But certainly because there is ready to hand a bound and unfree, rebellious but serviceable, black population against which Dunbar and all white men are enabled to measure these privileging and privileged differences.

Eventually individualism fuses with the prototype of Americans as solitary, alienated, and malcontent. What, one wants to ask, are Americans alienated from? What are Americans always so insistently innocent of? Different from? As for absolute power, over whom is this power held, from whom withheld, to whom distributed?

Answers to these questions lie in the potent and ego-reinforcing presence of an Africanist population. This population is convenient in every way, not the least of which is self-definition. This new white male can now persuade himself that savagery is "out there." The lashes ordered (500 applied five times is 2500) are not one's own savagery; repeated and dangerous breaks for freedom are "puzzling" confirmations of black irrationality; the combination of Dean Swift's beatitudes and a life of regularized violence is civilized; and if the sensibilities are dulled enough, the rawness remains external.

These contradictions slash their way through the pages of

American literature. How could it be otherwise? As Dominick LaCapra reminds us, "Classic novels are not only worked over . . . by common contextual forces (such as ideologies) but also rework and at least partially work through those forces in critical and at times potentially transformative fashion." *

As for the culture, the imaginative and historical terrain upon which early American writers journeyed is in large measure shaped by the presence of the racial other. Statements to the contrary, insisting on the meaninglessness of race to the American identity, are themselves full of meaning. The world does not become raceless or will not become unracialized by assertion. The act of enforcing racelessness in literary discourse is itself a racial act. Pouring rhetorical acid on the fingers of a black hand may indeed destroy the prints, but not the hand. Besides, what happens in that violent, self-serving act of erasure to the hands, the fingers, the fingerprints of the one who does the pouring? Do they remain acid-free? The literature itself suggests otherwise.

Explicit or implicit, the Africanist presence informs in compelling and inescapable ways the texture of American literature. It is a dark and abiding presence, there for the literary imagination as both a visible and an invisible mediating force. Even, and especially, when American texts are not "about" Africanist presences or characters or narrative or idiom, the

* Dominick LaCapra, *History, Politics and the Novel* (Ithaca: Cornell University Press, 1987), p. 4.

shadow hovers in implication, in sign, in line of demarcation. It is no accident and no mistake that immigrant populations (and much immigrant literature) understood their "Americanness" as an opposition to the resident black population. Race, in fact, now functions as a metaphor so necessary to the construction of Americanness that it rivals the old pseudo-scientific and class-informed racisms whose dynamics we are more used to deciphering.

As a metaphor for transacting the whole process of Americanization, while burying its particular racial ingredients, this Africanist presence may be something the United States cannot do without. Deep within the word "American" is its association with race. To identify someone as a South African is to say very little; we need the adjective "white" or "black" or "colored" to make our meaning clear. In this country it is quite the reverse. American means white, and Africanist people struggle to make the term applicable to themselves with ethnicity and hyphen after hyphen after hyphen. Americans did not have a profligate, predatory nobility from which to wrest an identity of national virtue while continuing to covet aristocratic license and luxury. The American nation negotiated both its disdain and its envy in the same way Dunbar did: through a self-reflexive contemplation of fabricated, mythological Africanism. For the settlers and for American writers generally, this Africanist other became the means of thinking about body, mind, chaos, kindness, and love; provided the occasion for exercises in the absence of restraint, the presence of restraint, the contemplation of freedom and of aggression; permitted opportunities for the exploration of ethics and morality, for meeting the obligations of the social contract, for bearing the cross of religion and following out the ramifications of power.

Reading and charting the emergence of an Africanist persona in the development of a national literature is both a fascinating project and an urgent one, if the history and criticism of our literature is to become accurate. Emerson's plea for intellectual independence was like the offer of an empty plate that writers could fill with nourishment from an indigenous menu. The language no doubt had to be English, but the content of that language, its subject, was to be deliberately, insistently un-English and anti-European, insofar as it rhetorically repudiated an adoration of the Old World and defined the past as corrupt and indefensible. In the scholarship on the formation of an American character and the production of a national literature, a number of items have been catalogued. A major item to be added to the list must be an Africanist presence—decidedly not American, decidedly other.

The need to establish difference stemmed not only from the Old World but from a difference in the New. What was distinctive in the New was, first of all, its claim to freedom and, second, the presence of the unfree within the heart of the democratic experiment—the critical absence of democracy, its echo, shadow, and silent force in the political and intellectual activity of some not-Americans. The distinguishing features of the not-Americans were their slave status, their social status—and their color.

It is conceivable that the first would have self-destructed in a variety of ways had it not been for the last. These slaves, unlike many others in the world's history, were visible to a fault. And they had inherited, among other things, a long history on the meaning of color. It was not simply that this slave population had a distinctive color; it was that this color "meant" something. That meaning had been named and deployed by scholars from at least the moment, in the eighteenth century, when other and sometimes the same scholars started to investigate both the natural history and the inalienable rights of man—that is to say, human freedom.

One supposes that if Africans all had three eyes or one ear, the significance of that difference from the smaller but conquering European invaders would also have been found to have meaning. In any case, the subjective nature of ascribing value and meaning to color cannot be questioned this late in the twentieth century. The point for this discussion is the alliance between visually rendered ideas and linguistic utterances. And this leads into the social and political nature of received knowledge as it is revealed in American literature.

Knowledge, however mundane and utilitarian, plays about in linguistic images and forms cultural practice. Responding to culture—clarifying, explicating, valorizing, translating, transforming, criticizing—is what artists everywhere do, especially writers involved in the founding of a new nation. Whatever their personal and formally political responses to the inherent contradiction of a free republic deeply committed to slavery, nineteenth-century writers were mindful of the presence of black people. More important, they addressed, in more or less passionate ways, their views on that difficult presence.

The alertness to a slave population did not confine itself to the personal encounters that writers may have had. Slave narratives were a nineteenth-century publication boom. The press, the political campaigns, and the policy of various parties and elected officials were rife with the discourse of slavery and freedom. It would have been an *isolato* indeed who was unaware of the most explosive issue in the nation. How could one speak of profit, economy, labor, progress, suffragism, Christianity, the frontier, the formation of new states, the acquisition of new lands, education, transportation (freight and passengers), neighborhoods, the military—of almost anything a country concerns itself with—without having as a referent, at the heart of the discourse, at the heart of definition, the presence of Africans and their descendants?

It was not possible. And it did not happen. What did happen frequently was an effort to talk about these matters with a vocabulary designed to disguise the subject. It did not always succeed, and in the work of many writers disguise was never intended. But the consequence was a master narrative that spoke *for* Africans and their descendants, or *of* them. The legislator's narrative could not coexist with a response from the Africanist persona. Whatever popularity the slave narratives had—and they influenced abolitionists and converted antiabolitionists—the slave's own narrative, while freeing the narrator in many ways, did not destroy the master narrative. The master narrative could make any number of adjustments to keep itself intact.

Silence from and about the subject was the order of the day. Some of the silences were broken, and some were maintained by authors who lived with and within the policing narrative. What I am interested in are the strategies for maintaining the silence and the strategies for breaking it. How did the founding writers of young America engage, imagine, employ, and create an Africanist presence and persona? In what ways do these strategies explicate a vital part of American literature? How does excavating these pathways lead to fresh and more profound analyses of what they contain and how they contain it?

.   .   .

Let me propose some topics that need critical investigation.

First, the Africanist character as surrogate and enabler. In what ways does the imaginative encounter with Africanism enable white writers to think about themselves? What are the dynamics of Africanism's self-reflexive properties? Note, for instance, the way Africanism is used to conduct a dialogue concerning American space in *The Narrative of Arthur Gordon Pym*. Through the use of Africanism, Poe meditates on place as a means of containing the fear of borderlessness and trespass, but also as a means of releasing and exploring the desire for a limitless empty frontier. Consider the ways that Africanism in other American writers (Mark Twain, Melville,

Hawthorne) serves as a vehicle for regulating love and the imagination as defenses against the psychic costs of guilt and despair. Africanism is the vehicle by which the American self knows itself as not enslaved, but free; not repulsive, but desirable; not helpless, but licensed and powerful; not history-less, but historical; not damned, but innocent; not a blind accident of evolution, but a progressive fulfillment of destiny.

A second topic in need of critical attention is the way an Africanist idiom is used to establish difference or, in a later period, to signal modernity. We need to explicate the ways in which specific themes, fears, forms of consciousness, and class relationships are embedded in the use of Africanist idiom: how the dialogue of black characters is construed as an alien, estranging dialect made deliberately unintelligible by spellings contrived to disfamiliarize it; how Africanist language practices are employed to evoke the tension between speech and speechlessness; how it is used to establish a cognitive world split between speech and text, to reinforce class distinctions and otherness as well as to assert privilege and power; how it serves as a marker and vehicle for illegal sexuality, fear of madness, expulsion, self-loathing. Finally, we should look at how a black idiom and the sensibilities it has come to imply are appropriated for the associative value they lend to modernism—to being hip, sophisticated, ultra-urbane.

Third, we need studies of the technical ways in which an Africanist character is used to limn out and enforce the invention and implications of whiteness. We need studies that analyze the strategic use of black characters to define the goals and enhance the qualities of white characters. Such studies will reveal the process of establishing others in order to know them, to display knowledge of the other so as to ease and to order external and internal chaos. Such studies will reveal the process by which it is made possible to explore and penetrate one's own body in the guise of the sexuality, vulnerability, and anarchy of the other—and to control projections of anarchy with the disciplinary apparatus of punishment and largess.

Fourth, we need to analyze the manipulation of the Africanist narrative (that is, the story of a black person, the experience of being bound and/or rejected) as a means of meditation—both safe and risky—on one's own humanity. Such analyses will reveal how the representation and appropriation of that narrative provides opportunities to contemplate limitation, suffering, rebellion, and to speculate on fate and destiny. They will analyze how that narrative is used for discourse on ethics, social and universal codes of behavior, and assertions about and definitions of civilization and reason. Criticism of this type will show how that narrative is used in the construction of a history and a context for whites by positing history-lessness and context-lessness for blacks.

These topics surface endlessly when one begins to look carefully, without restraining, protective agenda beforehand. They seem to me to render the nation's literature a much more complex and rewarding body of knowledge.

Two examples may clarify: one a major American novel

that is both a source and a critique of romance as a genre; the other the fulfillment of the promise I made earlier to return to those mute white images of Poe's.

.   .   .

If we supplement our reading of *Huckleberry Finn,* expand it—release it from its clutch of sentimental nostrums about lighting out to the territory, river gods, and the fundamental innocence of Americanness—to incorporate its contestatory, combative critique of antebellum America, it seems to be another, fuller novel. It becomes a more beautifully complicated work that sheds much light on some of the problems it has accumulated through traditional readings too shy to linger over the implications of the Africanist presence at its center. We understand that, at a certain level, the critique of class and race is there, although disguised or enhanced by humor and naiveté. Because of the combination of humor, adventure, and the viewpoint of the naif, Mark Twain's readers are free to dismiss the critique, the contestatory qualities, of the novel and focus on its celebration of savvy innocence, at the same time voicing polite embarrassment over the symptomatic racial attitude it enforces. Early criticism (that is, the reappraisals in the 1950s that led to the reification of *Huckleberry Finn* as a great novel) missed or dismissed the social quarrel in that work because it appears to assimilate the ideological assumptions of its society and culture; because it is narrated in the voice and controlled by the gaze of a child-without-status—someone outside, marginal, and already "othered" by the middle-class society he loathes and seems never to envy; and because the novel masks itself in the comic, parodic, and exaggerated tall-tale format.

On this young but street-smart innocent, Huck, who is virginally uncorrupted by bourgeois yearnings, fury, and helplessness, Mark Twain inscribes a critique of slavery and the pretensions of the would-be middle class, a resistance to the loss of Eden and the difficulty of becoming a social individual. The agency, however, for Huck's struggle is the nigger Jim, and it is absolutely necessary (for reasons I tried to illuminate earlier) that the term *nigger* be inextricable from Huck's deliberations about who and what he himself is—or, more precisely, is not. The major controversies about the greatness or near greatness of *Huckleberry Finn* as an American (or even "world") novel exist as controversies because they forgo a close examination of the interdependence of slavery and freedom, of Huck's growth and Jim's serviceability within it, and even of Mark Twain's inability to continue, to explore the journey into free territory.

The critical controversy has focused on the collapse of the so-called fatal ending of the novel. It has been suggested that the ending is brilliant finesse that returns Tom Sawyer to the center stage where he should be. Or it is a brilliant play on the dangers and limitations of romance. Or it is a sad and confused ending to the book of an author who, after a long blocked period, lost narrative direction; who changed the serious adult focus back to a child's story out of disgust. Or the ending is a valuable learning experience for Jim and Huck for which we and they should be grateful. What is not stressed is that there is no way, given the confines of the novel, for Huck to mature into a moral human being *in America* without Jim. To let Jim go free, to let him enter the mouth of the Ohio River and pass into free territory, would be to abandon the whole premise of the book. Neither Huck nor Mark Twain can tolerate, in imaginative terms, Jim freed. That would blast the predilection from its mooring.

Thus the fatal ending becomes the elaborate deferment of a necessary and necessarily unfree Africanist character's escape, because freedom has no meaning to Huck or to the text without the specter of enslavement, the anodyne to individualism; the yardstick of absolute power over the life of another; the signed, marked, informing, and mutating presence of a black slave.

The novel addresses at every point in its structural edifice, and lingers over in every fissure, the slave's body and personality: the way it speaks, what passion legal or illicit it is prey to, what pain it can endure, what limits, if any, there are to its suffering, what possibilities there are for forgiveness, compassion, love. Two things strike us in this novel: the apparently limitless store of love and compassion the black man has for his white friend and white masters; and his assumption that the whites are indeed what they say they are, superior and adult. This representation of Jim as the visible other can be read as the yearning of whites for forgiveness and love, but the yearning is made possible only when it is understood that Jim has recognized his inferiority (not as

slave, but as black) and despises it. Jim permits his perse-
cutors to torment him, humiliate him, and responds to the
torment and humiliation with boundless love. The humiliation that Huck and Tom subject Jim to is baroque, endless,
foolish, mind-softening—and it comes *after* we have experienced Jim as an adult, a caring father and a sensitive man. If
Jim had been a white ex-convict befriended by Huck, the
ending could not have been imagined or written: because it
would not have been possible for two children to play so
painfully with the life of a white man (regardless of his class,
education, or fugitiveness) once he had been revealed to us as
a moral adult. Jim's slave status makes play and deferment
possible—but it also dramatizes, in style and mode of narration, the connection between slavery and the achievement (in
actual and imaginary terms) of freedom. Jim seems unasser-
tive, loving, irrational, passionate, dependent, inarticulate (except for the "talks" he and Huck have, long sweet talks we
are not privy to—but what did you talk about, Huck?). It is
not what Jim seems that warrants inquiry, but what Mark
Twain, Huck, and especially Tom need from him that should
solicit our attention. In that sense the book may indeed be
"great" because in its structure, in the hell it puts its readers
through at the end, the frontal debate it forces, it simulates
and describes the parasitical nature of white freedom.

.   .   .

Forty years earlier, in the works of Poe, one sees how the
concept of the American self was similarly bound to Afri-

canism, and was similarly covert about its dependency. We can look to "The Gold-Bug" and "How to Write a Blackwood Article" (as well as *Pym*) for samples of the desperate need of this writer with pretensions to the planter class for the literary techniques of "othering" so common to American literature: estranging language, metaphoric condensation, fetishizing strategies, the economy of stereotype, allegorical foreclosure; strategies employed to secure his characters' (and his readers') identity. But there are unmanageable slips. The black slave Jupiter is said to whip his master in "The Gold-Bug"; the black servant Pompey stands mute and judgmental at the antics of his mistress in "A Blackwood Article." And Pym engages in cannibalism *before* he meets the black savages; when he escapes from them and witnesses the death of a black man, he drifts toward the silence of an impenetrable, inarticulate whiteness.

We are reminded of other images at the end of literary journeys into the forbidden space of blackness. Does Faulkner's *Absalom! Absalom!*, after its protracted search for the telling African blood, leave us with just such an image of snow and the eradication of race? Not quite. Shreve sees himself as the inheritor of the blood of African kings; the snow apparently is the wasteland of unmeaning, unfathomable whiteness. Harry's destiny and death dream in Hemingway's Africa is focused on the mountain top "great, high, and unbelievably white in the sun" in "The Snows of Kilimanjaro." *To Have and Have Not* closes with an image of a white boat. William Styron begins and ends Nat Turner's journey with a white, floating marble structure, windowless, doorless, incoherent. In *Henderson the Rain King* Saul Bellow ends the hero's journey to and from his fantastic Africa on the ice, the white frozen wastes. With an Africanist child in his arms, the soul of the Black King in his baggage, Henderson dances, he shouts, over the frozen whiteness, a new white man in a new found land: "leaping, pounding, and tingling over the pure white lining of the gray Arctic silence."

If we follow through on the self-reflexive nature of these encounters with Africanism, it falls clear: images of blackness can be evil *and* protective, rebellious *and* forgiving, fearful *and* desirable—all of the self-contradictory features of the self. Whiteness, alone, is mute, meaningless, unfathomable, pointless, frozen, veiled, curtained, dreaded, senseless, implacable. Or so our writers seem to say.

3
disturbing nurses and the kindness of sharks

But there was
a special hell besides
where black women lie waiting
for a boy—

William Carlos Williams
from "Adam"

*R*ace has become metaphorical—a way of referring to and disguising forces, events, classes, and expressions of social decay and economic division far more threatening to the body politic than biological "race" ever was. Expensively kept, economically unsound, a spurious and useless political asset in election campaigns, racism is as healthy today as it was during the Enlightenment. It seems that it has a utility far beyond economy, beyond the sequestering of classes from one another, and has assumed a metaphorical life so completely embedded in daily discourse that it is perhaps more necessary and more on display than ever before.

I am prepared to be corrected on this point insofar as it misrepresents the shelf life of racism in social and political behavior. But I remain convinced that the metaphorical and metaphysical uses of race occupy definitive places in American literature, in the "national" character, and ought to be a major concern of the literary scholarship that tries to know it.

In this last chapter I wish to observe and trace the transformation of American Africanism from its simplistic, though menacing, purposes of establishing hierarchic difference to its surrogate properties as self-reflexive meditations on the loss of difference, to its lush and fully blossomed existence in the rhetoric of dread and desire.

My suggestion that Africanism has come to have a metaphysical necessity should in no way be understood to imply that it has lost its ideological utility. There is still much ill-gotten gain to reap from rationalizing power grabs and clutches with inferences of inferiority and the ranking of differences. There is still much national solace in continuing dreams of democratic egalitarianism available by hiding class conflict, rage, and impotence in figurations of race. And there is quite a lot of juice to be extracted from plummy reminiscences of "individualism" and "freedom" if the tree upon which such fruit hangs is a black population forced to serve as freedom's polar opposite: individualism is foregrounded (and believed in) when its background is stereotypified, enforced dependency. Freedom (to move, to earn, to learn, to be allied with a powerful center, to narrate the world) can be relished more deeply in a cheek-by-jowl existence with the bound and unfree, the economically oppressed, the marginalized, the silenced. The ideological dependence on racialism is intact and, like its metaphysical existence, offers in historical, political, and literary discourse a safe route into meditations on morality and ethics; a way of examining the mind-body dichotomy; a way of thinking about justice; a way of contemplating the modern world.

Surely, it will be said, white America has considered questions of morality and ethics, the supremacy of mind and the vulnerability of body, the blessings and liabilities of progress and modernity, without reference to the situation of its black population. After all, it will be argued, where does one find a fulsome record that such a referent was part of these deliberations? My answer to these questions is another: where is it not?

In what public discourse does the reference to black people not exist? It exists in every one of this nation's mightiest struggles. The presence of black people is not only a major referent in the framing of the Constitution, it is also in the battle over enfranchising unpropertied citizens, women, the illiterate. It is there in the construction of a free and public school system; the balancing of representation in legislative bodies; jurisprudence and legal definitions of justice. It is there in theological discourse; the memoranda of banking houses; the concept of manifest destiny and the preeminent narrative that accompanies (if it does not precede) the initiation of every immigrant into the community of American citizens. The presence of black people is inherent, along with gender and family ties, in the earliest lesson every child is taught regarding his or her distinctiveness. Africanism is inextricable from the definition of Americanness—from its origins on through its integrated or disintegrating twentieth-century self.

The literature of the United States, like its history, represents commentary on the transformations of biological, ideological, and metaphysical concepts of racial difference. But the literature has an additional concern and subject matter: the private imagination interacting with the external world it inhabits. Literature redistributes and mutates in figurative language the social conventions of Africanism. In minstrelsy, a layer of blackness applied to a white face released it from law. Just as entertainers, through or by association with blackface, could render permissible topics that otherwise would have been taboo, so American writers were able to employ an imagined Africanist persona to articulate and imaginatively act out the forbidden in American culture.

Encoded or explicit, indirect or overt, the linguistic responses to an Africanist presence complicate texts, sometimes contradicting them entirely. A writer's response to American Africanism often provides a subtext that either sabotages the surface text's expressed intentions or escapes them through a language that mystifies what it cannot bring itself to articulate but still attempts to register. Linguistic responses to Africanism serve the text by further problematizing its matter with resonances and luminations. They can serve as allegorical fodder for the contemplation of Eden, expulsion, and the availability of grace. They provide paradox, ambiguity; they strategize omissions, repetitions, disruptions, polarities, reifications, violence. In other words, they give the text a deeper, richer, more complex life than the sanitized one commonly presented to us.

In his book on Faulkner, James Snead comments that racial divisions "show their flaws best in written form":

"Racism might be considered a normative recipe for domination created by speakers using rhetorical tactics. The characteristic figures of racial division repeat on the level of phoneme, sentence, and story: (1) The fear of merging, or loss of identity through synergistic union with the other, leads to the wish to use racial purification as a separating strategy against difference; (2) Marking, or supplying physically significant (usually visual) characteristics with internal value equivalents, sharpening, by visual antithesis, their conceptual utility; (3) Spatial and conceptual separation, often facilitated through unequal verbal substitutions that tend to omit and distance a subordinate class from realms of value and esteem; (4) Repetition, or pleonastic reinforcement of these antitheses in writing, storytelling, or hearsay; (5) Invective and threat, exemplified in random and unpredictable violence to punish real or imagined crimes; (6) Omission and concealment of the process by a sort of paralepsis that claims discrimination to be self-evidently valid and natural."

"Faulkner," he goes on to say, "counters these social figures with literary devices of his own." *

Following Snead's helpful categories, it may be useful to list some of the common linguistic strategies employed in fiction to engage the serious consequences of blacks.

1. Economy of stereotype. This allows the writer a quick and easy image without the responsibility of specificity, accuracy, or even narratively useful description.

* James A. Snead, *Figures of Division: William Faulkner's Major Novels* (New York: Methuen, 1986), pp. x–xi.

2. Metonymic displacement. This promises much but delivers little and counts on the reader's complicity in the dismissal. Color coding and other physical traits become metonyms that displace rather than signify the Africanist character.

3. Metaphysical condensation. This allows the writer to transform social and historical differences into universal differences. Collapsing persons into animals prevents human contact and exchange; equating speech with grunts or other animal sounds closes off the possibility of communication.

4. Fetishization. This is especially useful in evoking erotic fears or desires and establishing fixed and major difference where difference does not exist or is minimal. Blood, for example, is a pervasive fetish: black blood, white blood, the purity of blood; the purity of white female sexuality, the pollution of African blood and sex. Fetishization is a strategy often used to assert the categorical absolutism of civilization and savagery.

5. Dehistoricizing allegory. This produces foreclosure rather than disclosure. If difference is made so vast that the civilizing process becomes indefinite—taking place across an unspecified infinite amount of time—history, as a process of becoming, is excluded from the literary encounter. Flannery O'Connor's "The Artificial Nigger" makes this point with reference to Mr. Head's triumphantly racist views in that brilliant story. Carson McCullers deploys allegory among her characters in *The Heart Is a Lonely Hunter,* to mourn the inevitability of closure and the fruitlessness of monologue. Melville uses allegorical formations—the white whale, the

racially mixed crew, the black-white pairings of male couples, the questing, questioning white male captain who confronts impenetrable whiteness—to investigate and analyze hierarchic difference. Poe deploys allegorical mechanisms in *Pym* not to confront and explore, as Melville does, but to evade and simultaneously register the cul de sac, the estrangement, the non-sequitur that is entailed in racial difference. William Styron opens and closes *The Confessions of Nat Turner* with the sealed white structure that serves as an allegorical figuration of the defeat of the enterprise he is engaged in: penetration of the black-white barrier.

6. Patterns of explosive, disjointed, repetitive language. These indicate a loss of control in the text that is attributed to the objects of its attention rather than to the text's own dynamics.

I have gone on at some length about these linguistic strategies because I want to make use of them in a specific connection.

.   .   .

My interest in Ernest Hemingway becomes heightened when I consider how much apart his work is from African-Americans. That is, he has no need, desire, or awareness of them either as readers of his work or as people existing anywhere other than in his imaginative (and imaginatively lived) world. I find, therefore, his use of African-Americans much more artless and unselfconscious than Poe's, for example, where social unease required the servile black bodies in his work.

Hemingway's work could be described as innocent of nineteenth-century ideological agenda as well as free of what may be called recent, postmodernist sensitivity. With this in mind, a look at how Hemingway's fiction is affected by an Africanist presence—when it makes the writing belie itself, contradict itself, or depend on that presence for attempts at resolution—can be taken by way of a "pure" case to test some of the propositions I have been advancing.

I begin with the novel said by many to be intentionally political, *To Have and Have Not* (published in 1937). Harry Morgan, the central figure, seems to represent the classic American hero: a solitary man battling a government that would limit his freedom and his individuality. He is romantically and sentimentally respectful of the nature he destroys for a living (deep-sea fishing)—competent, street-wise, knowing, and impatient with those who are not. He is virile, risk-taking, risk-loving, and so righteous and guiltless in his evaluation of himself that it seems a shame to question or challenge it. Before I do challenge it, I want to examine how Hemingway shows the reader that Harry is knowing, virile, free, brave, and moral.

Only ten pages into the novel we encounter the Africanist presence. Harry includes a "nigger" in his crew, a man who, throughout all of part one, has no name. His appearance is signaled by the sentence, "Just then this nigger we had getting bait comes down the dock." The black man is not only nameless for five chapters, he is not even hired, just someone "we had getting bait"—a kind of trained response, not an agent possessing a job. His inclusion on the voyage, objected to by the white client, Johnson, is defended by Harry on the basis of the black man's skill: he "put on a nice bait and he was fast." The rest of the time, we are told, this nameless man sleeps and reads the papers.

Something very curious happens to this namelessness when, in part two, the author shifts voices. Part one is told in the first person, and whenever Harry thinks about this black man he thinks "nigger." In part two, where Hemingway uses the third-person point of view in narrating and representing Harry's speech, two formulations of the black man occur: he both remains nameless and stereotyped and becomes named and personalized.

Harry *says* "Wesley" when speaking to the black man in direct dialogue; Hemingway *writes* "nigger" when as narrator he refers to him. Needless to report, this black man is never identified as one (except in his own mind). Part two reserves and repeats the word "man" for Harry. The spatial and conceptual difference is marked by the shortcut that the term "nigger" allows, with all of its color and caste implications. The term occupies a territory between man and animal and thus withholds specificity even while marking it. This black character either does not speak (as a "nigger" he is silent) or speaks in very legislated and manipulated ways (as a "Wesley" his speech serves Harry's needs). Enforcing the silence of the "nigger" proves problematic in this action-narrative and requires of Hemingway some strenuous measures.

In part one, at a crucial moment during the fishing expedition, which has disappointed both the captain and his customer, the boat moves into promising waters. Harry is coaching Johnson; the black man is at the wheel. Earlier Harry assured us that the black man does nothing aside from cutting bait but read and sleep. But Hemingway realizes that Harry cannot be in two critical places at the same time, instructing the incompetent Johnson and guiding the vessel. It is important to remember that there is another person aboard, an alcoholic named Eddy, who is too unreliable to be given the responsibility of steering but who is given manhood and speech and a physical description. Eddy is white, and we know he is because nobody says so. Now, with Harry taking care of his customer and Eddy in a pleasant stupor, there is only the black man to tend the wheel.

When the sign heralding the promising waters arrives—the sighting of flying fish beyond the prow of the boat—the crewman facing forward ought to be the first to see them. In fact he is. The problem is how to acknowledge that first sighting and continue the muzzling of this "nigger" who, so far, has not said one word. The solution is a strangely awkward, oddly constructed sentence: "The nigger was still taking her out and I looked and saw he had seen a patch of flying fish burst out ahead."* "Saw he had seen" is improbable in syntax, sense, and tense but, like other choices available to Hemingway, it is risked to avoid a speaking black. The problem this

*Ernest Hemingway, *To Have and Have Not* (New York: Grosset and Dunlap, 1937), p. 13; subsequent quotations are from pp. 7–8, 68–70, 75, 87, 86, 258, 259, 113.

writer gives himself, then, is to say how one sees that someone else has already seen.

A better, certainly more graceful choice would be to have the black man cry out at the sighting. But the logic of the narrative's discrimination prevents a verbal initiative of importance to Harry's business coming from this nameless, sexless, nationless Africanist presence. It is the powerful one, the authoritative one, who sees. The power of looking is Harry's; the passive powerlessness is the black man's, though he himself does not speak of it. Silencing him, refusing him the opportunity of one important word, forces the author to abandon his search for transparency in the narrative act and to set up a curiously silent mate-captain relationship.

What would have been the cost, I wonder, of humanizing, genderizing, this character at the opening of the novel? For one thing, Harry would be positioned—set off, defined—very differently. He would have to be compared to a helpless alcoholic, a contemptible customer, and an individualized crew member with, at least by implication, an independent life. Harry would lack the juxtaposition and association with a vague presence suggesting sexual excitement, a possible threat to his virility and competence, violence under wraps. He would, finally, lack the complementarity of a figure who can be assumed to be in some way bound, fixed, unfree, and serviceable.

The proximity to violence is stressed at once in the novel, before the black crewman's entrance, by the shooting outside the café. The Cubans in this scene are separated not by nationality (all the people born in Cuba are Cubans) but as black and not black, Cubans and blacks. In this slaughter the blacks are singled out as the most gratuitously violent and savage. Hemingway writes:

> "The nigger with the Tommy gun got his face almost into the street and gave the back of the wagon a burst from underneath and sure enough one came down . . . at ten feet the nigger shot him in the belly with the Tommy gun, with what must have been the last shot . . . old Pancho sat down hard and went over forwards. He was trying to come up, still holding onto the Luger, only he couldn't get his head up, when the nigger took the shotgun that was lying against the wheel of the car by the chauffeur and blew the side of his head off. Some nigger."

In part two, Harry and the black crewman do engage in dialogue, and the black man talks a great deal. The service-ability of the black man's speech, however, is transparent. What he says and when he says it are plotted to win admiration for Harry. Wesley's speech is restricted to grumbles and complaints and apologies for weakness. We hear the grumbles, the groans, the weakness as Wesley's responses to his gunshot wounds for three pages before we learn that Harry is also shot, and much worse than Wesley is. By contrast, Harry has not only not mentioned his own pain, he has taken Wesley's whining with compassion and done the difficult work of steering and tossing the contraband overboard in swift, stoic gestures of manliness. Information about Harry's more serious pain is deferred while we listen to Wesley:

> "I'm shot . . ."
> "You're just scared."
> "No, sir. I'm shot. And I'm hurting bad. I've been throbbing all night." . . .
> "I hurt," the nigger said. "I hurt worse all the time."
> "I'm sorry, Wesley," the man said. "But I got to steer."
> "You treat a man no better than a dog," the nigger said. He was getting ugly now. But the man was still sorry for him.

Finally, our patience and Harry's exhausted, we get this exchange: "'Who the hell's shot worse?' he asked him. 'You or me?' 'You're shot worse,' the nigger said."

The choice and positioning of the naming process ("nigger," "Wesley," and, once, "negro") may seem arbitrary and confusing, but in fact it is carefully structured. Harry, in dialogue with a helpmate, cannot say "nigger" without offending the reader (if not the helpmate)—and losing his claim to compassionate behavior—so he uses a name. No such responsibility is taken on, however, by the legislating narrator, who always uses the generic and degrading term: "The nigger blubbered with his face against a sack. The man went on slowly lifting the sacked packages of liquor and dropping them over the side." Once Wesley has apologized, recognized, and accepted his inferiority, Harry can and does use "nigger," along with the proper name, in direct dialogue—in familiar camaraderie: "'Mr. Harry,' said the nigger, 'I'm sorry I couldn't help dump that stuff.' 'Hell,' said Harry, 'ain't no nigger any good when he's shot. You're a all right nigger, Wesley.'"

I mentioned two main categories of speech for the black man: grumbles and apology. But there is a third. Throughout the exchange, while the two men are suffering—one stoically, one whimperingly—the black man criticizes the white man in lapses between his whining and his terror. They are interesting lapses because they limn another Harry—a figure of antihuman negation and doom. Such lapses occur over and over again in Hemingway's fiction. Accusations of inhumanity, used as prophecies of doom, are repeatedly placed in the mouths of the blacks who people his work. "Ain't a man's life worth more than a load of liquor?" Wesley asks Harry. "Why don't people be honest and decent and make a decent honest living? . . . You don't care what happens to a man . . . You ain't hardly human." "'You ain't human,'" the nigger said. 'You ain't got human feelings.'"

.   .   .

The serviceability of the Africanist presence I have been describing becomes even more pronounced when Hemingway begins to describe male and female relationships. In this same novel, the last voice we hear is that of Harry's devoted wife, Marie, listing and celebrating the virtues, the virility and bravery, of her husband, who is now dead. The elements of her reverie can be schematically organized as follows: (1) virile, good, brave Harry; (2) racist views of Cuba; (3) black sexual invasion thwarted; (4) reification of whiteness.

Marie recalls him fondly as "snotty and strong and quick, and like some kind of expensive animal. It would always get me to just watch him move." Immediately following this encomium to sexuality and power and revered (expensive) brutality, she meditates on her hatred of Cubans (the Cubans killed Harry) and says they are "bad luck for Conchs" and "bad luck for anybody. They got too many niggers there too." This judgment is followed by her recollection of a trip she and Harry took to Havana when she was twenty-six years old. Harry had a lot of money then and while they walked in the park a "nigger" (as opposed to a Cuban, though the black man she is referring to is both black and Cuban), "said something" to Marie. Harry smacked him and threw his straw hat into the street where a taxi ran over it.

Marie remembers laughing so hard it made her belly ache. With nothing but a paragraph indention between them, the next reverie is a further association of Harry with sexuality, power, and protection. "That was the first time I ever made my hair blonde." The two anecdotes are connected in time and place and, significantly, by color as sexual coding. We do not know what the black man said, but the horror is that he said anything at all. It is enough that he spoke, claimed an intimacy perhaps, but certainly claimed a view and inserted his sexual self into their space and their consciousness. By initiating the remark, he was a speaking, therefore aggressive, presence. In Marie's recollection, sexuality, violence, class, and the retribution of an impartial machine are fused into an all-purpose black man.

The couple, Marie and Harry, is young and in love with obviously enough money to feel and be powerful in Cuba. Into that Eden comes the violating black male making impertinent remarks. The disrespect, with its sexual overtones, is punished at once by Harry's violence. He smacks the black man. Further, he picks up the fallen straw hat, violating the black man's property, just as the black man had sullied Harry's property—his wife. When the taxi, inhuman, onrushing, impartial machine, runs over the hat, it is as if the universe were rushing to participate in and validate Harry's response. It is this underscoring that makes Marie laugh—along with her obvious comfort in and adulation of this "strong and quick" husband of hers.

What follows in the beauty parlor is positioned as connected with and dependent on the episode of black invasion of privacy and intimation of sexuality from which Marie must be protected. The urgency to establish difference—a difference within the sexual context—is commanding. Marie tells us how she is transformed from black to white, from dark to blond. It is a painful and difficult process that turns out to be well worth the pain in its sexual, protective, differentiating payout: "They were working on it all afternoon and it was naturally so dark they didn't want to do it . . . but I kept telling them to see if they couldn't make it a little lighter . . . and all I'd say was, just see if you can't make it a little lighter."

When the bleaching and perming are done, Marie's satisfaction is decidedly sensual, if not explicitly sexual: "when I put my hand and touched it, and I couldn't believe it was me and I was so excited I was choked with it . . . I was so excited feeling all funny inside, sort of faint like." It is a genuine transformation. Marie becomes a self she can hardly believe, golden and soft and silky.

Her own sensual reaction to her whitening is echoed by Harry, who sees her and says, "Jesus, Marie, you're beautiful." And when she wants to hear more about her beauty, he tells her not to talk—just "Let's go to the hotel." This enhanced sexuality comes on the heels of a sexual intrusion by a black man.

What would have been the consequence if the insult to Marie had come from a white man? Would the bleaching have followed? If so, would it have been in such lush and sexually heightened language? What does establishing a difference from darkness to lightness accomplish for the concept of a self as sexually alive and potent? Or so powerful and coherent in the world?

These tourists in Havana meet a native of that city and have a privileged status because they are white. But to assure us that this status is both deserved and, by implication, potently generative, they encounter a molesting, physically inferior black male (his inferiority is designated by the fact that Harry does not use his fists, but slaps him) who represents the outlaw sexuality that, by comparison, spurs the narrative on to contemplation of a superior, legal, white counterpart.

Here we see Africanism used as a fundamental fictional technique by which to establish character. Within a milieu that threatens the dissolution of all distinctions of value— the milieu of the working poor, the unemployed, sinister Chinese, terrorist Cubans, violent but cowardly blacks, upper-class castrati, female predators—Harry and Marie (an ex-prostitute) gain potency, a generative sexuality. They solicit our admiration by the comparison that is struck between their claims to fully embodied humanity and a discredited Africanism. The voice of the text is complicit in these formulations: Africanism becomes not only a means of displaying authority but, in fact, constitutes its source.

.   .   .

The strategies that employ and distribute Africanism in *To Have and Have Not* become more sophisticated in the other work by Ernest Hemingway I will discuss here. In the posthumously published *The Garden of Eden* ideological Africanism is extended metaphorically to function as a systematic articulation, through an Africanist discursive practice and an Africanist mythology, of an entire aesthetics. Africanism— the fetishizing of color, the transference to blackness of the power of illicit sexuality, chaos, madness, impropriety, anarchy, strangeness, and helpless, hapless desire—provides a formidable field for a novel that works out the terms and maps a complete, if never formalized, aesthetics. Before describing this aesthetic field, I would like to mention one of the author's special concerns.

Hemingway's romantic attachment to a nurse is well documented in the fiction, in criticism, in biographical data, and more recently in the published recollection of the original nurse herself. The wounded soldier and the nurse is a familiar story and contains elements reliably poignant. To be in a difficult, even life-threatening position and to have someone dedicated to helping you, paid to help you, is soothing. And if you are bent on dramatic gestures of self-reliance, eager to prove that you can go it alone (without complaining), a nurse who chooses or is paid to take care of you does not violate your view of yourself as a brave, silent sufferer. Needfulness does not enter the picture; asking for help is always out of the question, and the benefits that derive from the attentive, expert care do not incur emotional debt.

Some of the other women in Hemingway's fiction who become objects of desire have the characteristics of nurses without the professional status. They are essentially the good wives or the good lovers, ministering, thoughtful, never needing to be told what the loved man needs. Such perfect nurses are rare, though important because they serve as a reference toward which the prose yearns. More common are the women who abandon or have difficulty sustaining their nursing abilities: women who destroy the silent sufferer, hurt him instead of nurturing him.

But in the exclusively male world that Hemingway usually prefers to inhabit, it would be missing something not to notice that there are nurse figures in the masculine domain as well. These characters are just as dedicated, thoughtful, and ministering of the narrator's needs as the few female nurses are. Some of these male nurses are explicitly, forthrightly tender helpers—with nothing to gain from their care but the most minimal wage or the pleasure of a satisfied patient. Other male nurses serve the narrator reluctantly, sullenly, but are excessively generous in the manner in which they serve the text. Cooperative or sullen, they are Tontos all, whose role is to do everything possible to serve the Lone Ranger without disturbing his indulgent delusion that he is indeed alone.

The reference is pertinent here, for not only is the Hemingway Ranger invariably accompanied but his Tontos, his nursemen, are almost always black. From the African bearers who tote the white man's burden in the hunting grounds of Africa, to the bait cutters aboard fishing boats, to loyal companions of decaying boxers, to ministering bartenders—the array of enabling black nursemen is impressive.

Along with their enabling properties are some disabling ones. They say—once their rank and status are signaled by the narrator and accepted by the black man—extraordinary things. Sam, the black man in "The Killers," tells Nick that "little boys always know what they want to do," scorning and dismissing what Nick takes on as his responsibility, commenting with derision on Nick's manhood. Wesley tells Harry Morgan, "You ain't hardly human." Bearers tell Francis Macomber that the lion is alive, and the buffalo too. Bugs in "The Battler" is described as a "gentle-voiced, crazy black man." According to Kenneth Lynn, Bugs "mothers" Ad, the ex-fighter deformed by his profession, "cooking him delicious fried ham and egg sandwiches and referring to him with unfailing politeness as Mister Francis. But the solicitous Negro is also a sadist, as the worn black leather on the blackjack he carries silently testifies. Master as well as slave, destroyer as well as caretaker, this black man is another of Hemingway's dark mother figures."* Although this critic uses the label "mother," he is extrapolating not the biological relationship but the caretaking, nursing characteristic inherent in the term. When Ad gets unmanageable, Bugs smashes him with his blackjack. (Remember the slave Jupiter in Poe's "Gold-Bug" who has similar leave to whip his master.) Bugs has also been given the gift of prophecy: "He says he's never been crazy," Ad tells Bugs. Bugs replies, "He's got a lot coming to him." Lynn notes that, in the late 1950s, Hemingway would reveal to a friend "an astonishing touchiness about these ominous words, as though he considered them to be a prophecy fulfilled."

No matter if they are loyal or resistant nurses, nourishing

---

*Kenneth S. Lynn, *Hemingway* (New York: Simon and Schuster, 1987), pp. 272–273.

and bashing the master's body, these black men articulate the narrator's doom and gainsay the protagonist-narrator's construction of himself. They modify his self-image; they violate the nurse's primary function of providing balm. In short, they disturb, in subtle and forceful ways, the narrator's construction of reality. We are left, as readers, wondering what to make of such prophecies, these slips of the pen, these clear and covert disturbances. And to wonder, as well, why they are placed so frequently in the mouths of black men.

It is as if the nurse were quite out of control. The other side of nursing, the opposite of the helping, healing hand, is the figure of destruction—the devouring predator whose inhuman and indifferent impulses pose immediate danger. Never still, always hungry, these figures are nevertheless seductive, elusive, and theatrical in their combination of power and deceit, love and death.

The devouring properties are given to women like Mrs. Macomber, women who slaughter their mates rather than see them in control and strongly independent. Hemingway describes the wife in "The Snows of Kilimanjaro" as "this kindly caretaker and destroyer of his talent." The black male nurses may verbalize destruction and doom, deny and contradict manliness, introduce and represent antagonism, but the Africanist codes keep them bound to their nursing function. The female nurses—as wives and lovers with caretaking as their primary role—give voice to and complete acts of destruction. They are predators, sharks, unnatural women who combine the signs of a nurse with those of the shark.

This combination brings us back for a moment to *To Have and Have Not.*

During a passionate scene of lovemaking, when even the stump of Harry's arm is in sexual play, Marie asks her husband:

"Listen, did you ever do it with a nigger wench?"
"Sure."
"What's it like?"
"Like nurse shark."

This extraordinary remark is saved and savored for Hemingway's description of a black female. The strong notion here is that of a black female as the furthest thing from human, so far away as to be not even mammal but fish. The figure evokes a predatory, devouring eroticism and signals the antithesis to femininity, to nurturing, to nursing, to replenishment. In short, Harry's words mark something so brutal, contrary, and alien in its figuration that it does not belong to its own species and cannot be spoken of in language, in metaphor or metonym, evocative of anything resembling the woman to whom Harry is speaking—his wife Marie. The kindness he has done Marie is palpable. His projection of black female sexuality has provided her with solace, for which she is properly grateful. She responds to the kindness and giggles, "You're funny."

It would be irresponsible and unjustified to invest Hemingway with the thoughts of his characters. It is Harry who thinks a black woman is like a nurse shark, not Hemingway. An author is not personally accountable for the acts of his fictive creatures, although he is responsible for them. And there is no evidence I know of to persuade me that Hemingway shared Harry's views. In point of fact there is strong evidence to suggest the opposite.

In *The Garden of Eden* Catherine, the wife of the narrator/protagonist David Bourne, spends all her days tanning, and clearly requires this darkening process for complex reasons other than cosmetic. Early in the novel, David interrogates her about what appears to him, and to us, an obsession with the aesthetics of her body:

> "Why do you want to be so dark?"
>
> "I don't know. Why do you want anything? Right now it's the thing that I want most. That we don't have I mean. Doesn't it make you excited to have me getting so dark?"
>
> "Uh-huh. I love it."
>
> "Did you think I could ever be this dark?"
>
> "No, because you're blond."
>
> "I can because I'm lion color and they can go dark. But I want every part of me dark and it's getting that way and you'll be darker than an Indian and that takes us further away from other people. You see why it's important."*

---

*Ernest Hemingway, *The Garden of Eden* (New York: Charles Scribner's Sons, 1986), p. 30; subsequent quotations are from pp. 177–178, 64, 29.

Catherine well understands the association of blackness with strangeness, with taboo—understands also that blackness is something one can "have" or appropriate; it's the one thing they lack, she tells him. Whiteness here is a deficiency. She comprehends how this acquisition of blackness "others" them and creates an ineffable bond between them—unifying them within the estrangement. When this lack is overcome, it is taken to be an assertion. The effect is heightened by Catherine's accompanying obsession with blonding her hair. Both of these coloring gestures—blackening up and whiting out—are codes Catherine imposes on David (inscribes on his body and places in his mind) to secure the sibling-twin emphasis that produces further sexual excitement.

The couple is not content with the brother-sister relationship; they require the further accent of twins, which the color coding, like the offprint of a negative, achieves. (This excitement of brother-sister incest is also the story the black man Bugs in "The Battler" tells Nick to explain why Ad went crazy: Ad's marriage dissolved after rumors that his wife was his sister.)

That story, acted out by a blacked-up couple in *The Garden of Eden,* is marked and stressed in its forbiddenness. Its voluptuous illegality is enforced by the associations constantly made between darkness and desire, darkness and irrationality, darkness and the thrill of evil. "Devil things," "night things," are Hemingway's descriptions of David and Catherine's appetites, and "Devil" becomes Catherine's nickname. "Just look at me," she says, after they have both had bleaching and haircuts, "That's how you are . . . And we're damned now. I was and now you are. Look at me and see how much you like it."

The remarkable and overt signs of brother-sister incest and of cross gender have occupied most of the published criticism of this novel. Unremarked is the Africanist field in which the drama is played out. Echoing Marie's tryst in the beauty parlor compelled by the specter of black sexuality she has just encountered, Catherine persuades herself that, while she needs regular hair whitening, she no longer needs tanning. "I don't really wear it," she says. "It's me. I really am this dark. The sun just develops it."

Catherine is both black and white, both male and female, and descends into madness once Marita appears, the "real" nurse, with dedicated, normal nursing functions. And it should be noted that Marita is naturally dark, with skin like the Javanese, a woman given to David by Catherine as a healing balm. The figurative gift that Harry gives Marie is analyzed and reformulated here: Catherine the shark gives David a dark nurse as an act of kindness. Her own nursing capabilities—her breasts—she calls her dowry. What is new and powerful and *hers* is the bleached white male-cut hair. It is a change Hemingway describes as "dark magic."

"When we go to Africa I want to be your African girl too," Catherine tells him. While we are not sure of exactly what this means to her, we are sure of what Africa means to him. Its availability as a blank, empty space into which he asserts himself, an uncreated void ready, waiting, and offering itself up for his artistic imagination, his work, his fiction, is unmistakable.

At the heart of *The Garden of Eden* is "Eden": the story David is writing about his adventures in Africa. It is a tale replete with male bonding, a father-son relationship, and even the elephant they track is loyal to his male companion. This fictional, Africanized Eden is sullied by the surrounding events of the larger Catherine-David Africanist Eden. Africa, imagined as innocent and under white control, is the inner story; Africanism, imagined as evil, chaotic, impenetrable, is the outer story.

The inner story Catherine despises and eventually destroys. She thinks it boring, irrelevant. David ought to be writing about her instead. The reader is made to understand and be repelled by her selfish narcissism. But in fact she is right. At least Hemingway thinks she is, for the story we are reading and the one he has written *is* about her. The African story David is struggling to write (and is able to write when Marita, the authentic dark nurse, takes over) is an old, familiar myth, Africa-as-Eden before and after its fall, where, as in "The Snows of Kilimanjaro," one goes to "work the fat off [one's] soul."

That story, which Catherine burns up, has value as a cherished masculine enclave of white domination and slaughter, complete with African servants who share David's "guilt and knowledge." But the narrative that encloses it, the blacked-up, Africanist one, comments thoroughly on an aestheticized blackness and a mythologized one. Both are fantastic. Both are pulled from fields of desire and need. Both are enabled by the discursive Africanism at the author's disposal.

.   .   .

I wish to close by saying that these deliberations are not about a particular author's attitudes toward race. That is another matter. Studies in American Africanism, in my view, should be investigations of the ways in which a nonwhite, Africanist presence and personae have been constructed—invented—in the United States, and of the literary uses this fabricated presence has served. In no way do I mean investigation of what might be called racist or nonracist literature, and I take no position, nor do I encourage one, on the quality of a work based on the attitudes of an author or whatever representations are made of some group. Such judgments can and are being formed, of course. Recent critical scholarship on Ezra Pound, Céline, T. S. Eliot, and Paul de Man comes to mind. But such concerns are not the intent of this exercise (although they fall within its reach). My project is an effort to avert the critical gaze from the racial object to the racial subject; from the described and imagined to the describers and imaginers; from the serving to the served.

Ernest Hemingway, who wrote so compellingly about what it was to be a white male American, could not help folding into his enterprise of American fiction its Africanist properties. But it would be a pity if the criticism of that literature continued to shellac those texts, immobilizing their complexities and power and luminations just below its tight, reflecting surface. All of us, readers and writers, are bereft when criticism remains too polite or too fearful to notice a disrupting darkness before its eyes.

Library of Congress Cataloging-in-Publication Data

Morrison, Toni.

Playing in the dark : whiteness and the literary imagination /
Toni Morrison.
  p. cm. — (The William E. Massey Sr. lectures in the history
of American civilization)
Includes bibliographical references.
ISBN 0-674-67377-8
1. American literature—White authors—History and criticism.
2. Afro-Americans in literature. 3. Blacks in literature.
4. Race in literature. I. Title. II. Series.
PS173.N4M67 1992
810.9'8034—dc20   91-39671
CIP

Playing in the Dark was designed by Gwen Frankfeldt

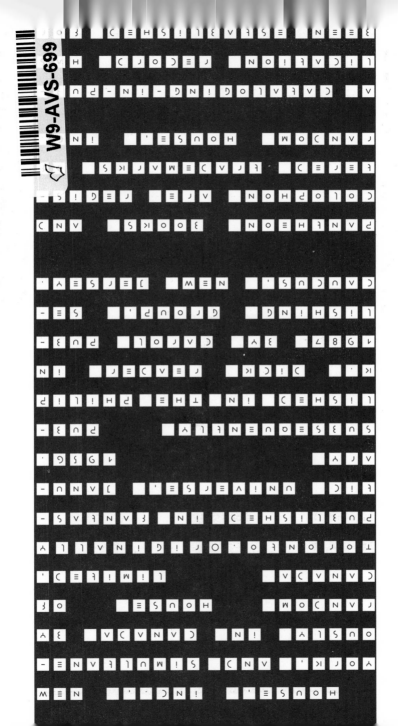

THE MINORITY REPORT

BY THE LIBRARY OF CONGRESS.

ISBN: 0-375-42187-4

WWW.PANTHEONBOOKS.COM

BOOK DESIGN BY CHIP KIDD

PRINTED IN MEXICO

FIRST EDITION

9 8 7 6 5 4 3 2 1

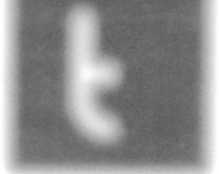

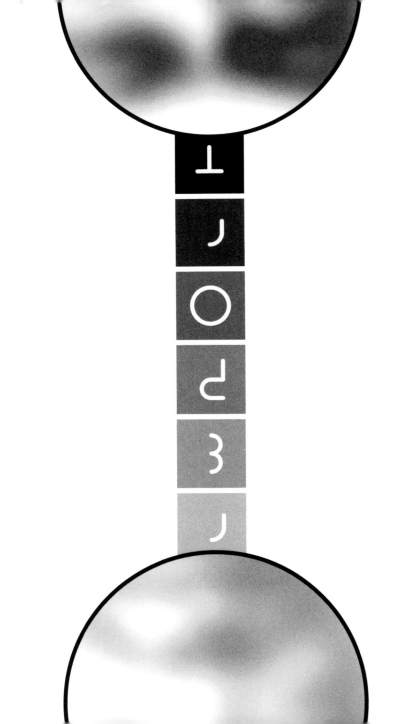

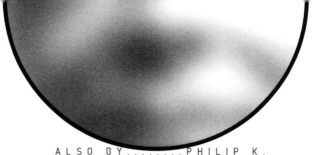

r e p o r t

PHILIP K.
DICK............PHILIP K.
PHILIP K.
DICK............PHILIP K.
DICK............PHILIP K.
DICK............PHILIP K.
DICK............
DICK............PHILIP K.
PHILIP K.
PHILIP K.
DICK............PHILIP K.
DICK............PHILIP K.
DICK............PHILIP K.
DICK............
DICK............PHILIP K.
DICK............PHILIP K.
DICK............PHILIP K.
DICK............
DICK............PHILIP K.
DICK............ DICK............PHILIP K.
DICK............PHILIP K.
DICK............
DICK............PHILIP K.
PHILIP K.

PANTHEON BOOKS * BOOKS * NEW * YORK

DICK............PHILIP K.
DICK............PHILIP K.
DICK............PHILIP K.

DESIGNED BY CHIP KIDD

DICK... DICK............PHILIP K.
DICK............PHILIP K.
DICK............
DICK............PHILIP K.
PHILIP K.
PHILIP K.

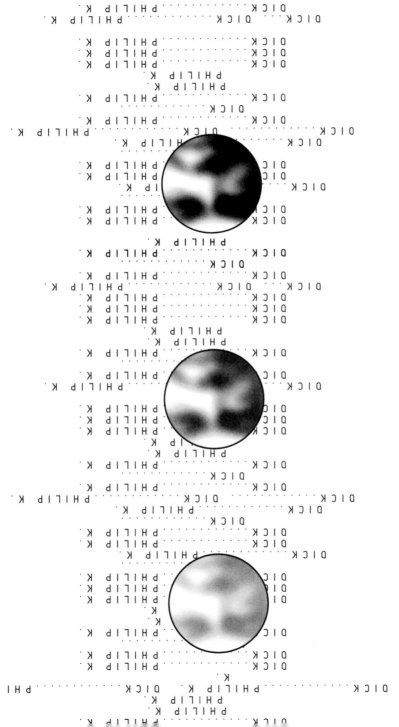

1

first thought Anderton had when he saw the young man was: *I'm getting bald. Bald and fat and old.* But he didn't say it aloud. Instead, he pushed back his chair, got to his feet, and came resolutely around the side of his desk, his right hand rigidly extended. Smiling with forced amiability, he shook hands with the young man.

"Witwer?" he asked, managing to make this query sound gracious.

"That's right," the young man said. "But the name's Ed to you, of course. That is, if you share my dislike for needless formality." The look on his blond, overly-confident face showed that he considered the matter settled. It would be Ed and John: Everything would be agreeably cooperative right from the start.

"Did you have much trouble finding the building?" Anderton asked guardedly, ignoring the too-friendly overture. *Good God, he had to hold on to something.* Fear touched him and he began to sweat. Witwer was moving around the office as if he already owned it—as if he were measuring it for size. Couldn't he wait a couple of days—a decent interval?

"No trouble," Witwer answered blithely, his hands in his pockets. Eagerly, he examined the voluminous files that lined the wall. "I'm not coming into your agency blind, you understand. I have quite a few ideas of my own about the way Precrime is run."

Shakily, Anderton lit his pipe. "How is it run? I should like to know."

"Not badly," Witwer said. "In fact, quite well."

Anderton regarded him steadily. "Is that your private opinion? Or is it just cant?"

Witwer met his gaze guilelessly. "Private and public. The Senate's pleased with your work. In fact, they're enthusiastic." He added, "As enthusiastic as very old men can be."

Anderton winced, but outwardly he remained impassive. It cost him an effort, though. He wondered what Witwer *really* thought. What was actually going on in that closecropped skull? The young man's eyes were blue, bright—and disturbingly clever. Witwer was nobody's fool. And obviously he had a great deal of ambition.

"As I understand it," Anderton said cautiously, "you're going to be my assistant until I retire."

"That's my understanding, too," the other replied, without an instant's hesitation.

"Which may be this year, or next year—or ten years from now." The pipe in Anderton's hand trembled. "I'm under no compulsion to retire. I founded Precrime and I can stay on here as long as I want. It's purely *my* decision."

Witwer nodded, his expression still guileless. "Of course."

With an effort, Anderton cooled down a trifle. "I merely wanted to get things straight."

"From the start," Witwer agreed. "You're the boss. What you say goes." With every evidence of sincerity, he asked: "Would you care to show me the organization? I'd like to familiarize myself with the general routine as soon as possible."

As they walked along the busy, yellow-lit tiers of offices, Anderton said: "You're acquainted with the theory of precrime, of course. I presume we can take that for granted."

"I have the information publicly available," Witwer replied. "With the aid of your precog mutants, you've boldly and successfully abolished the postcrime punitive system of jails and fines. As we all realize, punishment was never much of a deterrent, and could scarcely have afforded comfort to a victim already dead."

They had come to the descent lift. As it carried them swiftly downward, Anderton said: "You've probably grasped the basic legalistic drawback to precrime methodology. We're taking in individuals who have broken no law."

"But they surely will," Witwer affirmed with conviction.

"Happily they *don't*—because we get them first, before they can commit an act of violence. So the commission of the crime itself is absolute metaphysics. We claim they're culpable. They, on the other hand, eternally claim they're innocent. And, in a sense, they *are* innocent."

The lift let them out, and they again paced down a yellow corridor. "In our society we have no major crimes," Anderton went on, "but we do have a detention camp full of would-be criminals."

Doors opened and closed, and they were in the analytical wing. Ahead of them rose impressive banks of equipment—the data-receptors, and the computing mechanisms that studied and restructured the incoming material. And beyond the machinery sat the three precogs, almost lost to view in the maze of wiring.

"There they are," Anderton said dryly. "What do you think of them?"

In the gloomy half-darkness the three idiots sat babbling. Every incoherent utterance, every random syllable, was analyzed, compared, reassembled in the form of visual symbols, transcribed on conventional punchcards, and ejected into various coded slots. All day long the idiots babbled, imprisoned in their special high-backed chairs, held in one rigid position by metal bands, and bundles of wiring, clamps. Their physical needs were taken care of automatically. They had no spiritual needs. Vegetable-like, they muttered and dozed and existed. Their minds were dull, confused, lost in shadows.

But not the shadows of today. The three gibbering, fumbling creatures, with their enlarged heads and wasted bodies, were contemplating the future. The analytical machinery was recording prophecies, and as the three precog idiots talked, the machinery carefully listened.

For the first time Witwer's face lost its breezy confidence. A sick, dismayed expression crept into his eyes, a mixture of shame and moral shock. "It's not—pleasant," he murmured. "I didn't realize they were so—" He groped in his mind for the right word, gesticulating. "So—deformed."

"Deformed and retarded," Anderton instantly agreed. "Especially the girl, there. Donna is forty-five years old. But she looks about ten. The talent absorbs everything;

the esp-lobe shrivels the balance of the frontal area. But what do we care? We get their prophecies. They pass on what we need. They don't understand any of it, but *we* do."

Subdued, Witwer crossed the room to the machinery. From a slot he collected a stack of cards. "Are these names that have come up?" he asked.

"Obviously." Frowning, Anderton took the stack from him. "I haven't had a chance to examine them," he explained, impatiently concealing his annoyance.

Fascinated, Witwer watched the machinery pop a fresh card into the now empty slot. It was followed by a second— and a third. From the whirring disks came one card after another. "The precogs must see quite far into the future," Witwer exclaimed.

"They see a quite limited span," Anderton informed him. "One week or two ahead at the very most. Much of their data is worthless to us—simply not relevant to our line. We pass it on to the appropriate agencies. And they in turn trade data with us. Every important bureau has its cellar of treasured *monkeys.*"

"Monkeys?" Witwer stared at him uneasily. "Oh, yes, I understand. See no evil, speak no evil, et cetera. Very amusing."

"Very *apt.*" Automatically, Anderton collected the fresh cards which had been turned up by the spinning machinery. "Some of these names will be totally discarded. And most of the remainder record petty crimes: thefts, income tax evasion, assault, extortion. As I'm sure you know, Precrime has cut down felonies by ninety-nine and decimal point eight percent. We seldom get actual murder or treason. After all, the culprit knows we'll confine him in the detention camp a week before he gets a chance to commit the crime."

"When was the last time an actual murder was committed?" Witwer asked.

"Five years ago," Anderton said, pride in his voice.

"How did it happen?"

"The criminal escaped our teams. We had his name—in fact, we had all the details of the crime, including the victim's name. We knew the exact moment, the location of the planned act of violence. But in spite of us he was able to carry it out." Anderton shrugged. "After all, we can't get all of them." He riffled the cards. "But we do get most."

"One murder in five years." Witwer's confidence was returning. "Quite an impressive record . . . something to be proud of."

Quietly Anderton said: "I *am* proud. Thirty years ago I worked out the theory— back in the days when the self-seekers were thinking in terms of quick raids on the stock market. I saw something legitimate ahead—something of tremendous social value."

He tossed the packet of cards to Wally Page, his subordinate in charge of the monkey block. "See which ones we want," he told him. "Use your own judgment."

As Page disappeared with the cards, Witwer said thoughtfully: "It's a big responsibility."

"Yes, it is," agreed Anderton. "If we let one criminal escape—as we did five years ago—we've got a human life on our conscience. We're solely responsible. If we slip up, somebody dies." Bitterly, he jerked three new cards from the slot. "It's a public trust."

"Are you ever tempted to—" Witwer hesitated. "I mean, some of the men you pick up must offer you plenty."

"It wouldn't do any good. A duplicate file of cards pops out at Army GHQ. It's check and balance. They can keep their eye on us as continuously as they wish." Anderton glanced briefly at the top card. "So even if we wanted to accept a—"

He broke off, his lips tightening.

"What's the matter?" Witwer asked curiously.

Carefully, Anderton folded up the top card and put it away in his pocket. "Nothing," he muttered. "Nothing at all."

The harshness in his voice brought a flush to Witwer's face. "You really don't like me," he observed.

"True," Anderton admitted. "I don't. But—"

He couldn't believe he disliked the young man that much. It didn't seem possible: it *wasn't* possible. Something was wrong. Dazed, he tried to steady his tumbling mind.

On the card was his name. Line one— an already accused future murderer! According to the coded punches, Precrime Commissioner John A. Anderton was going to kill a man—and within the next week.

With absolute, overwhelming conviction, he didn't believe it.

the outer office, talking to Page, stood
Anderton's slim and attractive young wife,
Lisa. She was engaged in a sharp, animated discussion of policy, and barely
glanced up as Witwer and her husband
entered.

"Hello, darling," Anderton said.

Witwer remained silent. But his pale
eyes flickered slightly as they rested on
the brown-haired woman in her trim

police uniform. Lisa was now an executive official of Precrime but once, Witwer knew, she had been Anderton's secretary.

Noticing the interest on Witwer's face Anderton paused and reflected. To plant the card in the machines would require an accomplice on the inside—someone who was closely connected with Precrime and had access to the analytical equipment. Lisa was an improbable element. But the possibility did exist.

Of course, the conspiracy could be large-scale and elaborate, involving far more than a "rigged" card inserted somewhere along the line. The original data itself might have been tampered with. Actually, there was no telling how far back the alteration went. A cold fear touched him as he began to see the possibilities. His original impulse—to tear open the machines and remove all the data—was uselessly primitive. Probably the tapes agreed with the card: He would only incriminate himself further.

He had approximately twenty-four

hours. Then, the Army people would check over their cards and discover the discrepancy. They would find in their files a duplicate of the card he had appropriated. He had only one of two copies, which meant that the folded card in his pocket might just as well be lying on Page's desk in plain view of everyone.

From outside the building came the drone of police cars starting out on their routine round-ups. How many hours would elapse before one of them pulled up in front of *his* house?

"What's the matter, darling?" Lisa asked him uneasily. "You look as if you've just seen a ghost. Are you all right?"

"I'm fine," he assured her.

Lisa suddenly seemed to become aware of Ed Witwer's admiring scrutiny. "Is this gentleman your new co-worker, darling?" she asked.

Warily, Anderton introduced his new associate. Lisa smiled in friendly greeting.

Did a covert awareness pass between them? He couldn't tell. God, he was beginning to suspect everybody—not only his wife and Witwer, but a dozen members of his staff.

"Are you from New York?" Lisa asked.

"No," Witwer replied. "I've lived most of my life in Chicago. I'm staying at a hotel—one of the big downtown hotels. Wait—I have the name written on a card somewhere."

While he self-consciously searched his pockets, Lisa suggested: "Perhaps you'd like to have dinner with us. We'll be working in close cooperation, and I really think we ought to get better acquainted."

Startled, Anderton backed off. What were the chances of his wife's friendliness being benign, accidental? Witwer would be present the balance of the evening, and would now have an excuse to trail along to Anderton's private residence. Profoundly disturbed, he turned impulsively, and moved toward the door.

"Where are you going?" Lisa asked, astonished.

"Back to the monkey block," he told her. "I want to check over some rather puzzling data tapes before the Army sees them." He was out in the corridor before she could think of a plausible reason for detaining him.

Rapidly, he made his way to the ramp at its far end. He was striding down the outside stairs toward the public sidewalk, when Lisa appeared breathlessly behind him.

"What on earth has come over you?" Catching hold of his arm, she moved quickly in front of him. "I *knew* you were leaving," she exclaimed, blocking his way. "What's wrong with you? Everybody thinks you're—" She checked herself. "I mean, you're acting so erratically."

People surged by them—the usual afternoon crowd. Ignoring them, Anderton pried his wife's fingers from his arm. "I'm getting out," he told her. "While there's still time."

"But—*why?*"

"I'm being framed—deliberately and maliciously. This creature is out to get my job. The Senate is getting at me *through* him."

Lisa gazed up at him, bewildered. "But he seems like such a nice young man."

"Nice as a water moccasin."

Lisa's dismay turned to disbelief. "I don't believe it. Darling, all this strain you've been under—" Smiling uncertainly, she faltered: "It's not really credible that Ed Witwer is trying to frame you. How could he, even if he wanted to? Surely Ed wouldn't—"

"Ed?"

"That's his name, isn't it?"

Her brown eyes flashed in startled, wildly incredulous protest. "Good heavens, you're suspicious of everybody. You actually believe I'm mixed up with it in some way, don't you?"

He considered. "I'm not sure."

She drew closer to him, her eyes accusing. "That's not true. You really believe it. Maybe you *ought* to go away for a few weeks. You desperately need a rest. All this tension and trauma, a younger man coming in. You're acting paranoiac. Can't you see that? People plotting against you. Tell me, do you have any actual proof?"

Anderton removed his wallet and took out the folded card. "Examine this carefully," he said, handing it to her.

The color drained out of her face, and she gave a little harsh, dry gasp.

"The set-up is fairly obvious," Anderton told her, as levelly as he could. "This will give Witwer a legal pretext to remove me right now. He won't have to wait until I resign." Grimly, he added: "They know I'm good for a few years yet."

"But—"

"It will end the check and balance system. Precrime will no longer be an independent agency. The Senate will control the police, and after that—" His lips tightened. "They'll absorb the Army too. Well, it's outwardly logical enough. *Of course* I feel hostility and resentment toward Witwer—*of course* I have a motive.

"Nobody likes to be replaced by a younger man, and find himself turned out to pasture. It's all really quite plausible— except that I haven't the remotest intention of killing Witwer. But I can't prove that. So what can I do?"

Mutely, her face very white, Lisa shook her head. "I—I don't know. Darling, if only—"

"Right now," Anderton said abruptly, "I'm going home to pack my things. That's about as far ahead as I can plan."

"You're really going to—to try to hide out?"

"I am. As far as the Centaurian-colony planets, if necessary. It's been done successfully before, and I have a twenty-four-hour start." He turned resolutely. "Go back inside. There's no point in your coming with me."

"Did you imagine I would?" Lisa asked huskily.

Startled, Anderton stared at her. "Wouldn't you?" Then with amazement, he murmured: "No, I can see you don't believe me. You still think I'm imagining all this." He jabbed savagely at the card. "Even with that evidence you still aren't convinced."

"No," Lisa agreed quickly, "I'm not. You didn't look at it closely enough, darling. Ed Witwer's name isn't on it."

Incredulous, Anderton took the card from her.

"Nobody says you're going to kill Ed Witwer," Lisa continued rapidly, in a thin, brittle voice. "The card *must* be genuine, understand? And it has nothing to do with Ed. He's not plotting against you and neither is anybody else."

Too confused to reply, Anderton stood studying the card. She was right. Ed

Witwer was not listed as his victim. On line five, the machine had neatly stamped another name.

LEOPOLD KAPLAN

Numbly, he pocketed the card. He had never heard of the man in his life.

house was cool and deserted, and almost immediately Anderton began making preparations for his journey. While he packed, frantic thoughts passed through his mind.

Possibly he was wrong about Witwer—but how could he be sure? In any event, the conspiracy against him was far more complex than he had realized. Witwer, in the over-all picture, might be merely an insignificant puppet animated by someone else—by some distant, indistinct figure only vaguely visible in the background.

It had been a mistake to show the card to Lisa. Undoubtedly, she would describe it in detail to Witwer. He'd never get off Earth, never have an opportunity to find out what life on a frontier planet might be like.

While he was thus preoccupied, a board creaked behind him. He turned from the bed, clutching a weather-stained winter sports jacket, to face the muzzle of a gray-blue A-pistol.

"It didn't take you long," he said, staring with bitterness at the tight-lipped, heavyset man in a brown overcoat who stood holding the gun in his gloved hand. "Didn't she even hesitate?"

The intruder's face registered no response. "I don't know what you're talking about," he said. "Come along with me."

Startled, Anderton laid down the sports jacket. "You're not from my agency? You're not a police officer?"

Protesting and astonished, he was hustled outside the house to a waiting limousine. Instantly three heavily armed men closed in behind him. The door slammed and the car shot off down the highway, away from the city. Impassive and remote, the faces around him jogged with the motion of the speeding vehicle as open fields, dark and somber, swept past.

Anderton was till trying futilely to grasp the implications of what had happened, when the car came to a rutted side road, turned off, and descended into a gloomy sub-surface garage. Someone shouted an order. The heavy metal lock grated shut and overhead lights blinked on. The driver turned off the car motor.

"You'll have reason to regret this," Anderton warned hoarsely, as they dragged him from the car. "Do you realize who I am?"

"We realize," the man in the brown overcoat said.

At gun-point, Anderton was marched upstairs, from the clammy silence of the garage into a deep-carpeted hallway. He was, apparently, in a luxurious private residence, set out in the war-devoured rural area. At the far end of the hallway he could make out a room—a book-lined study simply but tastefully furnished. In a circle of lamplight, his face partly in shadows, a man he had never met sat waiting for him.

As Anderton approached, the man nervously slipped a pair of rimless glasses in place, snapped the case shut, and moistened his dry lips. He was elderly, perhaps seventy or older, and under his arm was a slim silver cane. His body was thin, wiry, his attitude curiously rigid. What little hair he had was dusty brown—a carefully-smoothed sheen of neutral color above his pale, bony skull. Only his eyes seemed really alert.

"Is this Anderton?" he inquired querulously, turning to the man in the brown overcoat. "Where did you pick him up?"

"At his home," the other replied. "He was packing—as we expected."

The man at the desk shivered visibly. "Packing." He took off his glasses and jerkily returned them to their case. "Look here," he said bluntly to Anderton, "what's the matter with you? Are you hopelessly insane? How could you kill a man you've never met?"

The old man, Anderton suddenly realized, was Leopold Kaplan.

"First, I'll ask you a question," Anderton countered rapidly. "Do you realize what you've done? I'm Commissioner of Police. I can have you sent up for twenty years."

He was going to say more, but a sudden wonder cut him short.

"How did you find out?" he demanded. Involuntarily, his hand went to his pocket, where the folded card was hidden. "It won't be for another—"

"I wasn't notified through your agency,"

Kaplan broke in, with angry impatience. "The fact that you've never heard of me doesn't surprise me too much. Leopold Kaplan, General of the Army of the Federated Westbloc Alliance." Begrudgingly, he added. "Retired, since the end of the Anglo-Chinese War, and the abolishment of AFWA."

It made sense. Anderton had suspected that the Army processed its duplicate cards immediately, for its own protection. Relaxing somewhat, he demanded: "Well? You've got me here. What next?"

"Evidently," Kaplan said, "I'm not going to have you destroyed, or it would have shown up on one of those miserable little cards. I'm curious about you. It seemed incredible to me that a man of your stature could contemplate the cold-blooded murder of a total stranger. There must be something more here. Frankly, I'm puzzled. If it represented some kind of Police strategy—" He shrugged his thin shoulders. "Surely you wouldn't have permitted the duplicate card to reach us."

"Unless," one of his men suggested, "it's a deliberate plant."

Kaplan raised his bright, bird-like eyes and scrutinized Anderton. "What do you have to say?"

"That's exactly what it is," Anderton said, quick to see the advantage of stating frankly what he believed to be the simple truth. "The prediction on the card was deliberately fabricated by a clique inside the police agency. The card is prepared and I'm netted. I'm relieved of my authority automatically. My assistant steps in and claims he prevented the murder in the usual efficient Precrime manner. Needless to say, there is no murder or intent to murder."

"I agree with you that there will be no murder," Kaplan affirmed grimly. "You'll be in police custody. I intend to make certain of that."

Horrified, Anderton protested: "You're

31

taking me back there? If I'm in custody I'll never be able to prove—"

"I don't care what you prove or don't prove," Kaplan interrupted. "All I'm interested in is having you out of the way." Frigidly, he added: "For my own protection."

"He was getting ready to leave," one of the men asserted.

"That's right," Anderton said, sweating. "As soon as they get hold of me I'll be confined in the detention camp. Witwer will take over—lock, stock and barrel." His face darkened. "And my wife. They're acting in concert, apparently."

For a moment Kaplan seemed to waver. "It's possible," he conceded, regarding Anderton steadily. Then he shook his head. "I can't take the chance. If this is a frame against you, I'm sorry. But it's simply not my affair." He smiled slightly. "However, I wish you luck." To the men he said: "Take him to the police building and turn him over to the highest authority." He mentioned the name of the acting commissioner, and waited for Anderton's reaction.

"Witwer!" Anderton echoed, incredulous.

Still smiling slightly, Kaplan turned and clicked on the console radio in the study. "Witwer has already assumed authority. Obviously, he's going to create quite an affair out of this."

There was a brief static hum, and then, abruptly, the radio blared out into the room—a noisy professional voice, reading a prepared announcement.

". . . all citizens are warned not to shelter or in any fashion aid or assist this dangerous marginal individual. The extraordinary circumstance of an escaped criminal at liberty and in a position to commit an act of violence is unique in modern times. All citizens are hereby notified that legal statues still in force implicate any and all persons failing to cooperate fully with the police in their task of apprehending John Allison Anderton. To repeat: The Precrime Agency of the Federal Westbloc Government is in the process of locating and neutralizing its former Commissioner, John Allison Anderton, who, through the methodology of the precrime-system, is hereby declared a potential murderer and as such forfeits his rights to freedom and all its privileges."

"It didn't take him long," Anderton muttered, appalled. Kaplan snapped off the radio and the voice vanished.

"Lisa must have gone directly to him," Anderton speculated bitterly.

"Why should he wait?" Kaplan asked. "You made your intentions clear."

He nodded to his men. "Take him back to town. I feel uneasy having him so close. In that respect I concur with Commissioner Witwer. I want him neutralized as soon as possible."

light rain beat against the pavement, as the car moved through the dark streets of New York City toward the police building.

"You can see his point," one of the men said to Anderton. "If you were in his place you'd act just as decisively."

Sullen and resentful, Anderton stared straight ahead.

"Anyhow," the man went on, "you're just one of many. Thousands of people have gone to that detention camp. You won't be lonely. As a matter of fact, you may not want to leave."

Helplessly, Anderton watched pedestrians hurrying along the rain-swept sidewalks. He felt no strong emotion. He was aware only of an overpowering fatigue. Dully, he checked off the street numbers: they were getting near the police station.

"This Witwer seems to know how to take advantage of an opportunity," one of the men observed conversationally. "Did you ever meet him?"

"Briefly," Anderton answered.

"He wanted your job—so he framed you. Are you sure of that?"

Anderton grimaced. "Does it matter?"

"I was just curious." The man eyed him languidly. "So you're the ex-Commissioner of Police. People in the camp will be glad to see you coming. They'll remember you."

"No doubt," Anderton agreed.

"Witwer sure didn't waste any time. Kaplan's lucky—with an official like that in charge." The man looked at Anderton almost pleadingly. "You're really convinced it's a plot, eh?"

"Of course."

"You wouldn't harm a hair of Kaplan's head? For the first time in history, Precrime goes wrong? An innocent man is framed by one of those cards. Maybe there've been other innocent people—right?"

"It's quite possible," Anderton admitted listlessly.

"Maybe the whole system can break down. Sure, you're not going to commit a murder—and maybe none of them were. Is that why you told Kaplan you wanted to keep yourself outside? Were you hoping to prove the system wrong? I've got an open mind, if you want to talk about it."

Another man leaned over, and asked, "Just between the two of us, is there really anything to this plot stuff? Are you really being framed?"

Anderton sighed. At that point he

wasn't certain, himself. Perhaps he was trapped in a closed, meaningless time-circle with no motive and no beginning. In fact, he was almost ready to concede that he was the victim of a weary, neurotic fantasy, spawned by growing insecurity. Without a fight, he was willing to give himself up. A vast weight of exhaustion lay upon him. He was struggling against the impossible—and all the cards were stacked against him.

The sharp squeal of tires roused him. Frantically, the driver struggled to control the car, tugging at the wheel and slamming on the brakes, as a massive bread truck loomed up from the fog and ran directly across the lane ahead. Had he gunned the motor instead he might have saved himself. But too late he realized his error. The car skidded, lurched, hesitated for a brief instant, and then smashed head on into the bread truck.

Under Anderton the seat lifted up and flung him face-forward against the door. Pain, sudden, intolerable, seemed to burst in his brain as he lay gasping and trying feebly to pull himself to his knees. Somewhere the crackle of fire echoed dismally, a patch of hissing brilliance winking in the swirls of mist making their way into the twisted hulk of the car.

Hands from outside the car reached for him. Slowly he became aware that he was being dragged through the rent that had been the door. A heavy seat cushion was shoved brusquely aside, and all at once he found himself on his feet, leaning heavily against a dark shape and being guided into the shadows of an alley a short distance from the car.

In the distance, police sirens wailed.

"You'll live," a voice grated in his ear, low and urgent. It was a voice he had never heard before, as unfamiliar and harsh as the rain beating into his face. "Can you hear what I'm saying?"

"Yes," Anderton acknowledged. He plucked aimlessly at the ripped sleeve of his shirt. A cut on his cheek was beginning to throb. Confused, he tried to orient himself. "You're not—"

"Stop talking and listen." The man was heavyset, almost fat. Now his big hands held Anderton propped against the wet brick wall of the building, out of the rain and the flickering light of the burning car. "We had to do it that way," he said. "It was the only alternative. We didn't have much time. We thought Kaplan would keep you at his place longer."

"Who are you?" Anderton managed.

The moist, rain-streaked face twisted into a humorless grin. "My name's Fleming. You'll see me again. We have about five seconds before the police get here. Then we're back where we started." A flat packet was stuffed into Anderton's hands. "That's enough loot to keep you going. And there's a full set of identification in there. We'll contact you from time to time." His grin increased and became a nervous chuckle. "Until you've proved your point."

Anderton blinked. "It is a frameup, then?"

"Of course." Sharply, the man swore. "You mean they got you to believe it, too?"

"I thought—" Anderton had trouble talking; one of his front teeth seemed to be loose. "Hostility toward Witwer . . . replaced, my wife and a younger man, natural resentment. . . ."

"Don't kid yourself," the other said. "You know better than that. This whole business was worked out carefully. They had every phase of it under control. The card was set to pop the day Witwer appeared. They've already got the first part wrapped up. Witwer is Commissioner, and you're a hunted criminal."

"Who's behind it?"

"Your wife."

Anderton's head spun. "You're positive?"

The man laughed. "You bet your life." He glanced quickly around. "Here come the police. Take off down this alley. Grab a bus, get yourself into the slum section, rent a room and buy a stack of magazines to keep you busy. Get other clothes—You're smart enough to take care of yourself. Don't try to leave Earth. They've got all the intersystem transports screened. If you can keep low for the next seven days, you're made."

"Who are you?" Anderton demanded.

Fleming let go of him. Cautiously, he moved to the entrance of the alley and peered out. The first police car had come to rest on the damp pavement; its motor spinning tinnily, it crept suspiciously toward the smouldering ruin that had been Kaplan's car. Inside the wreck the squad of men were stirring feebly, beginning to creep painfully through the tangle of steel and plastic out into the cold rain.

"Consider us a protective society," Fleming said softly, his plump, expressionless face shining with moisture. "A sort of police force that watches the police. To see," he added, "that everything stays on an even keel."

His thick hand shot out. Stumbling, Anderton was knocked away from him, half-falling into the shadows and damp debris that littered the alley.

"Get going," Fleming told him sharply. "And don't discard that packet." As Anderton felt his way hesitantly toward the far exit of the alley, the man's last words drifted to him. "Study it carefully and you may still survive."

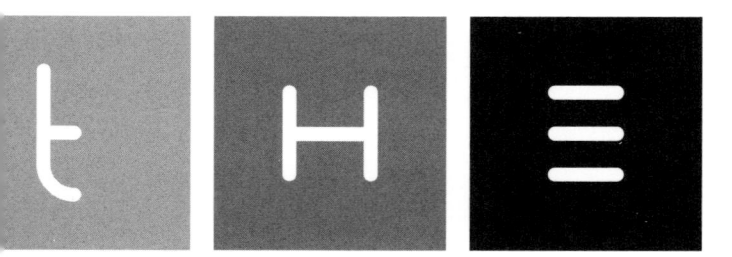

identification cards described him as Ernest Temple, an unemployed electrician, drawing a weekly subsistence from the State of New York, with a wife and four children in Buffalo and less than a hundred dollars in assets. A sweat-stained green card gave him permission to travel and to maintain no fixed address. A man looking for work needed to travel. He might have to go a long way.

As he rode across town in the almost empty bus, Anderton studied the description of Ernest Temple. Obviously, the cards had been made out with him in mind, for all the measurements fitted. After a time he wondered about the fingerprints and the brain-wave pattern. They couldn't possibly stand comparison. The walletful of cards would get him past only the most cursory examinations.

But it was something. And with the ID cards came ten thousand dollars in bills. He pocketed the money and cards, then turned to the neatly-typed message in which they had been enclosed.

At first he could make no sense of it. For a long time he studied it, perplexed.

> *The existence of a majority logically*
> *implies a corresponding minority.*

The bus had entered the vast slum region, the tumbled miles of cheap hotels and broken-down tenements that had sprung up after the mass destruction of the war. It slowed to a stop, and Anderton got to his feet. A few passengers idly observed his cut cheek and damaged clothing. Ignoring them, he stepped down onto the rain-swept curb.

Beyond collecting the money due him, the hotel clerk was not interested. Anderton climbed the stairs to the second floor and entered the narrow, musty-smelling room that now belonged to him. Gratefully, he locked the door and pulled down the window shades. The room was small but clean. Bed, dresser, scenic calendar, chair, lamp, a radio with a slot for the insertion of quarters.

He dropped a quarter into it and threw himself heavily down on the bed. All main stations carried the police bulletin. It was novel, exciting, something unknown to the present generation. An escaped criminal! The public was avidly interested.

". . . this man has used the advantage of his high position to carry out an initial escape," the announcer was saying, with professional indignation. "Because of his high office he had access to the previewed data and the trust placed in him permitted him to evade the normal process of detection and re-location. During the period of his tenure he exercised his authority to send countless potentially guilty individuals to their proper confinement, thus sparing the lives of innocent victims. This man, John Allison Anderton, was instrumental in the original creation of the Precrime system, the prophylactic pre-detection of criminals through the ingenious use of mutant precogs, capable of previewing future events and transferring orally that data to analytical machinery. These three precogs, in their vital function. . . ."

The voice faded out as he left the room and entered the tiny bathroom. There, he stripped off his coat, and shirt, and ran hot water in the wash bowl. He began bathing the cut on his cheek. At the drugstore on the corner he had bought iodine and Band-aids, a razor, comb, toothbrush, and other

small things he would need. The next
morning he intended to find a second-hand
clothing store and buy more suitable clothing. After all, he was now an unemployed
electrician, not an accident-damaged Commissioner of Police.

In the other room the radio blared on.
Only subconsciously aware of it, he stood
in front of the cracked mirror, examining a
broken tooth.

". . . the system of three precogs finds
its genesis in the computers of the middle
decades of this century. How are the
results of an electronic computer checked?
By feeding the data to a second computer
of identical design. But two computers are
not sufficient. If each computer arrived at
a different answer it is impossible to tell *a
priori* which is correct. The solution, based
on a careful study of statistical method, is
to utilize a third computer to check the
results of the first two. In this manner, a
so-called majority report is obtained. It
can be assumed with fair probability that
the agreement of two out of three comput-

ers indicates which of the alternative results is accurate. It would not be likely that two computers would arrive at identically incorrect solutions—"

Anderton dropped the towel he was clutching and raced into the other room. Trembling, he bent to catch the blaring words of the radio.

". . . unanimity of all three precogs is a hoped-for but seldom-achieved phenomenon, acting-Commissioner Witwer explains. It is much more common to obtain a collaborative majority report of two precogs, plus a minority report of some slight variation, usually with reference to time and place, from the third mutant. This is explained by the theory of *multiple-futures*. If only one time-path existed, precognitive information would be of no importance, since no possibility would exist, in possessing this information, of altering the future. In the Precrime Agency's work we must first of all assume—"

f r a n t i c a l l y

Frantically, Anderton paced around the tiny room. Majority report—only two of the precogs had concurred on the material underlying the card. That was the meaning of the message enclosed with the packet. The report of the third precog, the minority report, was somehow of importance.

Why?

His watch told him that it was after midnight. Page would be off duty. He wouldn't be back in the monkey block until the next afternoon. It was a slim chance, but worth taking. Maybe Page would cover for him, and maybe not. He would have to risk it.

He had to see the minority report.

BETWEEN

noon and one o'clock the rubbish-littered streets swarmed with people. He chose that time, the busiest part of the day, to make his call. Selecting a phonebooth in a patron-teeming super drugstore, he dialed the familiar police number and stood holding the cold receiver to his ear. Deliberately, he had selected the aud, not the vid line: in spite of his second-hand clothing and seedy, unshaven appearance, he might be recognized.

The receptionist was new to him. Cautiously, he gave Page's extension. If Witwer were removing the regular staff and putting in his satellites, he might find himself talking to a total stranger.

"Hello," Page's gruff voice came.

Relieved, Anderton glanced around. Nobody was paying any attention to him. The shoppers wandered among the merchandise, going about their daily routines. "Can you talk?" he asked. "Or are you tied up?"

There was a moment of silence. He could picture Page's mild face torn with uncertainty as he wildly tried to decide what to do. At last came halting words. "Why—are you calling here?"

Ignoring the question, Anderton said, "I didn't recognize the receptionist. New personnel?"

"Brand-new," Page agreed, in a thin, strangled voice. "Big turnovers, these days."

"So I hear." Tensely, Anderton asked, "How's your job? Still safe?"

"Wait a minute." The receiver was put down and the muffled sound of steps came in Anderton's ear. It was followed by the quick slam of a door being hastily shut. Page returned. "We can talk better now," he said hoarsely.

"How much better?"

"Not a great deal. Where are you?"

"Strolling through Central Park," Anderton said. "Enjoying the sunlight." For all he knew, Page had gone to make sure the line-tap was in place. Right now, an airborne police team was probably on its way. But he had to take the chance. "I'm in a new field," he said curtly. "I'm an electrician these days."

"Oh?" Page said, baffled.

"I thought maybe you had some work for me. If it can be arranged, I'd like to drop by and examine your basic computing

EQUIPMENT

equipment. Especially the data and analytical banks in the monkey block."

After a pause, Page said: "It—might be arranged. If it's really important."

"It is," Anderton assured him. "When would be best for you?"

"Well," Page said, struggling. "I'm having a repair team come in to look at the intercom equipment. The acting-Commissioner wants it improved, so he can operate quicker. You might trail along."

"I'll do that. About when?"

"Say four o'clock. Entrance B, level 6. I'll—meet you."

"Fine," Anderton agreed, already starting to hang up. "I hope you're still in charge, when I get there."

He hung up and rapidly left the booth. A moment later he was pushing through the dense pack of people crammed into the nearby cafeteria. Nobody would locate him there.

He had three and a half hours to wait. And it was going to seem a lot longer. It proved to be the longest wait of his life before he finally met Page as arranged.

The first thing Page said was: "You're out of your mind. Why in hell did you come back?"

"I'm not back for long." Tautly, Anderton prowled around the monkey block, systematically locking one door after another. "Don't let anybody in. I can't take chances."

"You should have quit when you were ahead." In an agony of apprehension, Page followed after him. "Witwer is making hay, hand over fist. He's got the whole country screaming for your blood."

Ignoring him, Anderton snapped open the main control bank of the analytical machinery. "Which of the three monkeys gave the minority report?"

"Don't question me—I'm getting out." On his way to the door Page halted briefly, pointed to the middle figure, and then disappeared. The door closed; Anderton was alone.

The middle one. He knew that one well. The dwarfed, hunched-over figure had sat buried in its wiring and relays for fifteen years. As Anderton approached, it didn't look up. With eyes glazed and blank, it contemplated a world that did not yet exist, blind to the physical reality that lay around it.

"Jerry" was twenty-four years old. Originally, he had been classified as a hydrocephalic idiot but when he reached the age of six the psych testers had identified the precog talent, buried under the layers of tissue corrosion. Placed in a government-operated training school, the latent talent had been cultivated. By the time he was nine the talent had advanced to a useful stage. "Jerry," however, remained in the aimless chaos of idiocy; the burgeoning faculty had absorbed the totality of his personality.

Squatting down, Anderton began disassembling the protective shields that guarded the tape-reels stored in the analytical machinery. Using schematics, he traced the leads back from the final stages of the integrated computers, to the point where "Jerry's" individual equipment branched off. Within minutes he was shakily lifting out two half-hour tapes: recent rejected data not fused with majority reports. Consulting the code chart, he selected the section of tape which referred to his particular card.

A tape scanner was mounted nearby. Holding his breath, he inserted the tape, activated the transport, and listened. It took only a second. From the first statement of the report it was clear what had happened. He had what he wanted; he could stop looking.

"Jerry's" vision was misphased. Because of the erratic nature of precognition, he was examining a time-area slightly different from that of his companions. For him, the report that Anderton would commit a murder was an event to be integrated along with everything else. That assertion—and Anderton's reaction—was one more piece of datum.

Obviously, "Jerry's" report superseded the majority report. Having been informed that he would commit a murder, Anderton would change his mind and not do so. The preview of the murder had cancelled out the murder; prophylaxis had occurred simply in his being informed. Already, a new time-path had been created. But "Jerry" was outvoted.

Trembling, Anderton rewound the tape and clicked on the recording head. At high speed he made a copy of the report, restored the original, and removed the duplicate from the transport. Here was the proof that the card was invalid: *obsolete.* All he had to do was show it to Witwer. . . .

His own stupidity amazed him. Undoubtedly, Witwer had seen the report; and in spite of it, had assumed the job of Commissioner, had kept the police teams out. Witwer didn't intend to back down;

he wasn't concerned with Anderton's innocence.

What, then, could he do? Who else would be interested?

"You damn fool!" a voice behind him grated, wild with anxiety.

Quickly, he turned. His wife stood at one of the doors, in her police uniform, her eyes frantic with dismay. "Don't worry," he told her briefly, displaying the reel of tape. "I'm leaving."

Her face distorted, Lisa rushed frantically up to him. "Page said you were here, but I couldn't believe it. He shouldn't have let you in. He just doesn't understand what you are."

"What am I?" Anderton inquired caustically. "Before you answer, maybe you better listen to this tape."

"I don't want to listen to it! I just want you to get out of here! Ed Witwer knows somebody's down here. Page is trying to keep him occupied, but—" She broke off, her head turned stiffly to one side. "He's here now! He's going to force his way in."

"Haven't you got any influence? Be gracious and charming. He'll probably forget about me."

Lisa looked at him in bitter reproach. "There's a ship parked on the roof. If you want to get away. . . ." Her voice choked and for an instant she was silent. Then she said, "I'll be taking off in a minute or so. If you want to come—"

"I'll come," Anderton said. He had no other choice. He had secured his tape, his proof, but he hadn't worked out any method of leaving. Gladly, he hurried after the slim figure of his wife as she strode from the block, through a side door and down a supply corridor, her heels clicking loudly in the deserted gloom.

"It's a good fast ship," she told him over her shoulder. "It's emergency-fueled—ready to go. I was going to supervise some of the teams."

the wheel of the high-velocity police cruiser, Anderton outlined what the minority report tape contained. Lisa listened without comment, her face pinched and strained, her hands clasped tensely in her lap. Below the ship, the war-ravaged rural countryside spread out like a relief map, the vacant regions between cities crater-pitted and dotted with the ruins of farms and small industrial plants.

"I wonder," she said, when he had finished, "how many times this has happened before."

"A minority report? A great many times."

"I mean, one precog misphased. Using the report of the others as data—superseding them." Her eyes dark and serious, she added, "Perhaps a lot of the people in the camps are like you."

"No," Anderton insisted. But he was beginning to feel uneasy about it, too. "I was in a position to see the card, to get a look at the report. That's what did it."

"But—" Lisa gestured significantly. "Perhaps all of them would have reacted that way. We could have told them the truth."

"It would have been too great a risk," he answered stubbornly.

Lisa laughed sharply. "Risk? Chance? Uncertainty? With precogs around?"

Anderton concentrated on steering the fast little ship. "This is a unique case," he repeated. "And we have an immediate problem. We can tackle the theoretical aspects later on. I have to get this tape to the proper people—before your bright young friend demolishes it."

"You're taking it to Kaplan?"

"I certainly am." He tapped the reel of tape which lay on the seat between them. "He'll be interested. Proof that his life isn't in danger ought to be of vital concern to him."

From her purse, Lisa shakily got out her cigarette case. "And you think he'll help you."

"He may—or he may not. It's a chance worth taking."

"How did you manage to go underground so quickly?" Lisa asked. "A completely effective disguise is difficult to obtain."

"All it takes is money," he answered evasively.

As she smoked, Lisa pondered. "Probably Kaplan will protect you," she said. "He's quite powerful."

"I thought he was only a retired general."

"Technically—that's what he is. But Witwer got out the dossier on him. Kaplan heads an unusual kind of exclusive veterans' organization. It's actually a kind of club, with a few restricted members. High officers only—an international class from both sides of the war. Here in New York they maintain a great mansion of a house, three glossy-paper publications, and occasional TV coverage that costs them a small fortune."

"What are you trying to say?"

"Only this. You've convinced me that you're innocent. I mean, it's obvious that you *won't* commit a murder. But you must realize now that the original report, the majority report, *was not a fake.* Nobody falsified it. Ed Witwer didn't create it. There's no plot against you, and there never was. If you're going to accept this minority report as genuine you'll have to accept the majority one, also."

Reluctantly, he agreed. "I suppose so."

"Ed Witwer," Lisa continued, "is acting

in complete good faith. He really believes you're a potential criminal—and why not? He's got the majority report sitting on his desk, but you have that card folded up in your pocket."

"I destroyed it," Anderton said, quietly.

Lisa leaned earnestly toward him. "Ed Witwer isn't motivated by any desire to get your job," she said. "He's motivated by the same desire that has always dominated you. He believes in Precrime. He wants the system to continue. I've talked to him and I'm convinced he's telling the truth."

Anderton asked, "Do you want me to take this reel to Witwer? If I do—he'll destroy it."

"Nonsense," Lisa retorted. "The originals have been in his hands from the start. He could have destroyed them any time he wished."

"That's true." Anderton conceded. "Quite possibly he didn't know."

"Of course he didn't. Look at it this way.

If Kaplan gets hold of that tape, the police will be discredited. Can't you see why? It would prove that the majority report was an error. Ed Witwer is absolutely right. You have to be taken in—if Precrime is to survive. You're thinking of your own safety. But think, for a moment, about the system." Leaning over, she stubbed out her cigarette and fumbled in her purse for another. "Which means more to you—your own personal safety or the existence of the system?"

"My safety," Anderton answered, without hesitation.

"You're positive?"

"If the system can survive only by imprisoning innocent people, then it deserves to be destroyed. My personal safety is important because I'm a human being. And furthermore—"

From her purse, Lisa got out an incredibly tiny pistol. "I believe," she told him huskily, "that I have my finger on the firing release. I've never used a weapon like this before. But I'm willing to try."

After a pause, Anderton asked: "You want me to turn the ship around? Is that it?"

"Yes, back to the police building. I'm sorry. If you could put the good of the system above your own selfish—"

"Keep your sermon," Anderton told her. "I'll take the ship back. But I'm not going to listen to your defense of a code of behavior no intelligent man could subscribe to."

Lisa's lips pressed into a thin, bloodless line. Holding the pistol tightly, she sat facing him, her eyes fixed intently on him as he swung the ship in a broad arc. A few loose articles rattled from the glove compartment as the little craft turned on a radical slant, one wing rising majestically until it pointed straight up.

Both Anderton and his wife were supported by the constraining metal arms of their seats. But not so the third member of the party.

Out of the corner of his eye, Anderton

saw a flash of motion. A sound came simultaneously, the clawing struggle of a large man as he abruptly lost his footing and plunged into the reinforced wall of the ship. What followed happened quickly. Fleming scrambled instantly to his feet, lurching and wary, one arm lashing out for the woman's pistol. Anderton was too startled to cry out. Lisa turned, saw the man—and screamed. Fleming knocked the gun from her hand, sending it clattering to the floor.

Grunting, Fleming shoved her aside and retrieved the gun. "Sorry," he gasped, straightening up as best he could. "I thought she might talk more. That's why I waited."

"You were here when—" Anderton began—and stopped. It was obvious that Fleming and his men had kept him under surveillance. The existence of Lisa's ship had been duly noted and factored in, and while Lisa had debated whether it would be wise to fly him to safety, Fleming had crept into the storage compartment of the ship.

"Perhaps," Fleming said, "you'd better give me that reel of tape." His moist, clumsy fingers groped for it. "You're right—Witwer would have melted it down to a puddle."

"Kaplan, too?" Anderton asked numbly, still dazed by the appearance of the man.

"Kaplan is working directly with Witwer. That's why his name showed on line five of the card. Which one of them is the actual boss, we can't tell. Possibly neither." Fleming tossed the tiny pistol away and got out his own heavy-duty military weapon. "You pulled a real flub in taking off with this woman. I told you she was back of the whole thing."

"I can't believe that," Anderton protested. "If she—"

"You've got no sense. This ship was warmed up by Witwer's order. They wanted to fly you out of the building so that we

COULDN'T

couldn't get to you. With you on your own, separated from us, you didn't stand a chance."

A strange look passed over Lisa's stricken features. "It's not true," she whispered. "Witwer never saw this ship. I was going to supervise—"

"You almost got away with it," Fleming interrupted inexorably. "We'll be lucky if a police patrol ship isn't hanging on us. There wasn't time to check." He squatted down as he spoke, directly behind the woman's chair. "The first thing is to get this woman out of the way. We'll have to drag you completely out of this area. Page tipped off Witwer on your new disguise, and you can be sure it has been widely broadcast."

Still crouching, Fleming seized hold of Lisa. Tossing his heavy gun to Anderton, he expertly tilted her chin up until her temple was shoved back against the seat. Lisa clawed frantically at him; a thin, terrified wail rose in her throat. Ignoring her,

Fleming closed his great hands around her neck and began relentlessly to squeeze.

"No bullet wound," he explained, gasping. "She's going to fall out—natural accident. It happens all the time. But in this case, her neck will be broken *first.*"

It seemed strange that Anderton waited so long. As it was, Fleming's thick fingers were cruelly embedded in the woman's pale flesh before he lifted the butt of the heavyduty pistol and brought it down on the back of Fleming's skull. The monstrous hands relaxed. Staggered, Fleming's head fell forward and he sagged against the wall of the ship. Trying feebly to collect himself, he began dragging his body upward. Anderton hit him again, this time above the left eye. He fell back, and lay still.

Struggling to breathe, Lisa remained for a moment huddled over, her body swaying back and forth. Then, gradually, the color crept back into her face.

"Can you take the controls?" Anderton asked, shaking her, his voice urgent.

"Yes, I think so." Almost mechanically she reached for the wheel. "I'll be all right. Don't worry about me."

"This pistol," Anderton said, "is Army ordnance issue. But it's not from the war. It's one of the useful new ones they've developed. I could be a long way off but there's just a chance—"

He climbed back to where Fleming lay spread out on the deck. Trying not to touch the man's head, he tore open his coat and rummaged in his pockets. A moment later Fleming's sweat-sodden wallet rested in his hands.

Tod Fleming, according to his identification, was an Army Major attached to the Internal Intelligence Department of Military Information. Among the various papers was a document signed by General Leopold Kaplan, stating that Fleming was under the special protection of his own group—the International Veterans' League.

Fleming and his men were operating

under Kaplan's orders. The bread truck, the accident, had been deliberately rigged.

It meant that Kaplan had deliberately kept him out of police hands. The plan went back to the original contact in his home, when Kaplan's men had picked him up as he was packing. Incredulous, he realized what had really happened. Even then, they were making sure they got him before the police. From the start, it had been an elaborate strategy to make certain that Witwer would fail to arrest him.

"You were telling the truth," Anderton said to his wife, as he climbed back in the seat. "Can we get hold of Witwer?"

Mutely, she nodded. Indicating the communications circuit of the dashboard, she asked: "What—did you find?"

"Get Witwer for me. I want to talk to him as soon as I can. It's very urgent."

Jerkily, she dialed, got the closed-channel mechanical circuit, and raised police headquarters in New York. A visual panorama of petty police officials flashed by before a tiny replica of Ed Witwer's features appeared on the screen.

"Remember me?" Anderton asked him.

Witwer blanched. "Good God. What happened? Lisa, are you bringing him in?" Abruptly his eyes fastened on the gun in Anderton's hands. "Look," he said savagely, "don't do anything to her. Whatever you may think, she's not responsible."

"I've already found that out," Anderton answered. "Can you get a fix on us? We may need protection getting back."

"Back!" Witwer gazed at him unbelievingly. "You're coming in? You're giving yourself up?"

"I am, yes." Speaking rapidly, urgently, Anderton added, "There's something you must do immediately. Close off the monkey block. Make certain nobody gets it—Page or anyone else. *Especially Army people.*"

"Kaplan," the miniature image said.

"What about him?"

"He was here. He—he just left."

Anderton's heart stopped beating. "What was he doing?"

"Picking up data. Transcribing duplicates of our precog reports on you. He insisted he wanted them solely for his protection."

"Then he's already got it," Anderton said. "It's too late."

Alarmed, Witwer almost shouted: "Just what do you mean? What's happening?"

"I'll tell you," Anderton said heavily, "when I get back to my office."

met him on the roof on the police building. As the small ship came to rest, a cloud of escort ships dipped their fins and sped off. Anderton immediately approached the blond-haired young man.

"You've got what you wanted," he told him. "You can lock me up, and send me to the detention camp. But that won't be enough."

Witwer's blue eyes were pale with uncertainty. "I'm afraid I don't understand—"

"It's not my fault. I should never have left the police building. Where's Wally Page?"

"We've already clamped down on him," Witwer replied. "He won't give us any trouble."

Anderton's face was grim.

"You're holding him for the wrong reason," he said. "Letting me into the monkey block was no crime. But passing information to Army is. You've had an Army plant working here." He corrected himself, a little lamely, "I mean, I have."

"I've called back the order on you. Now the teams are looking for Kaplan."

"Any luck?"

"He left here in an Army truck. We followed him, but the truck got into a militarized Barracks. Now they've got a big wartime R-3 tank blocking the street. It would be civil war to move it aside."

Slowly, hesitantly, Lisa made her way from the ship. She was still pale and

shaken and on her throat an ugly bruise was forming.

"What happened to you?" Witwer demanded. Then he caught sight of Fleming's inert form lying spread out inside. Facing Anderton squarely, he said: "Then you've finally stopped pretending this is some conspiracy of mine."

"I have."

"You don't think I'm—" He made a disgusted face. "*Plotting* to get your job."

"Sure you are. Everybody is guilty of that sort of thing. And I'm plotting to keep it. But this is something else—and you're not responsible."

"Why do you assert," Witwer inquired, "that it's too late to turn yourself in? My God, we'll put you in the camp. The week will pass and Kaplan will still be alive."

"He'll be alive, yes," Anderton conceded. "But he can prove he'd be just as alive if I were walking the streets. He has the information that proves the majority report obsolete. He can break the Precrime system." He finished, "Heads or tails, he wins—and we lose. The Army discredits us; their strategy paid off."

"But why are they risking so much? What exactly do they want?"

"After the Anglo-Chinese War, the Army lost out. It isn't what it was in the good old AFWA days. They ran the complete show, both military and domestic. And they did their own police work."

"Like Fleming," Lisa said faintly.

"After the war, the Westbloc was demilitarized. Officers like Kaplan were retired and discarded. Nobody likes that." Anderton grimaced. "I can sympathize with him. He's not the only one. But we couldn't keep on running things that way. We had to divide up the authority."

"You say Kaplan has won," Witwer said. "Isn't there anything we can do?"

"I'm not going to kill him. We know it and he knows it. Probably he'll come around and offer us some kind of deal. We'll continue to function, but the Senate will abolish our real pull. You wouldn't like that, would you?"

"I should say not," Witwer answered emphatically. "One of these days I'm going to be running this agency." He flushed. "Not immediately, of course."

Anderton's expression was somber. "It's too bad you publicized the majority report. If you had kept it quiet, we could cautiously draw it back in. But everybody's heard about it. We can't retract it now."

"I guess not," Witwer admitted awkwardly. "Maybe I—don't have this job down as neatly as I imagined."

"You will, in time. You'll be a good police officer. You believe in the status quo. But learn to take it easy." Anderton moved away from them. "I'm going to study the data tapes of the majority report. I want to find out exactly how I was supposed to kill Kaplan." Reflectively, he finished: "It might give me some ideas."

The data tapes of the precogs "Donna" and "Mike" were separately stored. Choosing the machinery responsible for the analysis of "Donna," he opened the protective shield and laid out the contents. As before, the code informed him which reels were relevant and in a moment he had the tape-transport mechanism in operation.

It was approximately what he had suspected. This was the material utilized by "Jerry"—the superseded time-path. In it Kaplan's Military Intelligence agents kidnapped Anderton as he drove home from work. Taken to Kaplan's villa, the organization GHQ of the International Veterans' League. Anderton was given an ultimatum: voluntarily disband the Precrime system or face open hostilities with Army.

In this discarded time-path, Anderton, as Police Commissioner, had turned to the Senate for support. No support was forthcoming. To avoid civil war, the Senate had ratified the dismemberment of the police system, and decreed a return to military law "to cope with the emergency." Taking a corps of fanatic police, Anderton had located Kaplan and shot him, along with other officials of the Veterans' League. Only Kaplan had died. The others had been patched up. And the coup had been successful.

This was "Donna." He rewound the tape and turned to the material previewed by "Mike." It would be identical; both pre-cogs had combined to present a unified picture. "Mike" began as "Donna" had begun: Anderton had become aware of Kaplan's plot against the police. But something was wrong. Puzzled, he ran the tape back to the beginning. Incomprehensibly, it didn't jibe. Again he relayed the tape, listening intently.

The "Mike" report was quite different from the "Donna" report.

An hour later, he had finished his examination, put away the tapes, and left the monkey block. As soon as he emerged, Witwer asked. "What's the matter? I can see something's wrong."

"No," Anderton answered slowly, still deep in thought. "Not exactly wrong." A sound came to his ears. He walked vaguely over to the window and peered out.

The street was crammed with people. Moving down the center lane was a four-column line of uniformed troops. Rifles, helmets . . . marching soldiers in their dingy wartime uniforms, carrying the cherished pennants of AFWA flapping in the cold afternoon wind.

"An Army rally," Witwer explained bleakly. "I was wrong. They're not going to make a deal with us. Why should they? Kaplan's going to make it public."

Anderton felt no surprise. "He's going to read the minority report?"

"Apparently. They're going to demand the Senate disband us, and take away our authority. They're going to claim we've been arresting innocent men—nocturnal police raids, that sort of thing. Rule by terror."

"You suppose the Senate will yield?"

Witwer hesitated. "I wouldn't want to guess."

"I'll guess," Anderton said. "They will. That business out there fits with what I learned downstairs. We've got ourselves boxed in and there's only one direction we can go. Whether we like it or not, we'll have to take it." His eyes had a steely glint.

Apprehensively, Witwer asked: "What is it?"

"Once I say it, you'll wonder why you didn't invent it. Very obviously, I'm going to have to fulfill the publicized report. I'm going to have to kill Kaplan. That's the only way we can keep them from discrediting us."

"But," Witwer said, astonished, "the majority report has been superseded."

"I can do it," Anderton informed him, "but it's going to cost. You're familiar with the statutes governing first-degree murder?"

"Life imprisonment."

"At least. Probably, you could pull a few wires and get it commuted to exile. I could be sent to one of the colony planets, the good old frontier."

"Would you—prefer that?"

"Hell, no," Anderton said heartily. "But it would be the lesser of the two evils. And it's got to be done."

"I don't see how you can kill Kaplan."

Anderton got out the heavy-duty military weapon Fleming had tossed to him. "I'll use this."

"They won't stop you?"

"Why should they? They've got that minority report that says I've changed my mind."

"Then the minority report is incorrect?"

"No," Anderton said, "it's absolutely correct. But I'm going to murder Kaplan anyhow."

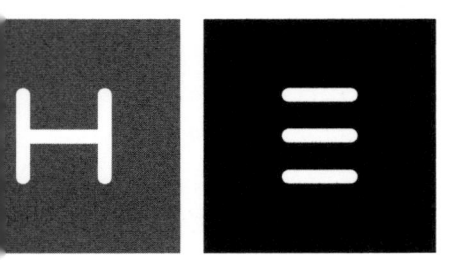

had never killed a man. He had never even seen a man killed. And he had been Police Commissioner for thirty years. For this generation, deliberate murder had died out. It simply didn't happen.

A police car carried him to within a block of the Army rally. There, in the shadows of the back seat, he painstakingly examined the pistol Fleming had provided him. It seemed to be intact. Actually, there was no doubt of the outcome. He was absolutely certain of what would happen within the next half hour. Putting the pistol back together, he opened the door of the parked car and stepped warily out.

Nobody paid the slightest attention to him. Surging masses of people pushed eagerly forward, trying to get within hearing distance of the rally. Army uniforms predominated and at the perimeter of the cleared area, a line of tanks and major weapons was displayed—formidable armament still in production.

Army had erected a metal speaker's stand and ascending steps. Behind the stand hung the vast AFWA banner, emblem of the combined powers that had fought in the war. By a curious corrosion of time, the AFWA Veterans' League included officers from the wartime enemy. But a general was a general and fine distinctions had faded over the years.

Occupying the first rows of seats sat the high brass of the AFWA command. Behind them came junior commissioned

officers

officers. Regimental banners swirled in a variety of colors and symbols. In fact, the occasion had taken on the aspect of a festive pageant. On the raised stand itself sat stern-faced dignitaries of the Veterans' League, all of them tense with expectancy. At the extreme edges, almost unnoticed, waited a few police units, ostensibly to keep order. Actually, they were informants making observations. If order were kept, the Army would maintain it.

The late-afternoon wind carried the muffled booming of many people packed tightly together. As Anderton made his way through the dense mob he was engulfed by the solid presence of humanity. An eager sense of anticipation held everybody rigid. The crowd seemed to sense that something spectacular was on the way. With difficulty, Anderton forced his way past the rows of seats and over to the tight knot of Army officials at the edge of the platform.

Kaplan was among them. But he was now General Kaplan.

The vest, the gold pocket watch, the cane, the conservative business suit—all were gone. For this event, Kaplan had got his old uniform from its mothballs. Straight and impressive, he stood surrounded by what had been his general staff. He wore his service bars, his medals, his boots, his decorative short-sword, and his visored cap. It was amazing how transformed a bald man became under the stark potency of an officer's peaked and visored cap.

Noticing Anderton, General Kaplan broke away from the group and strode to where the younger man was standing. The expression on his thin, mobile countenance showed how incredulously glad he was to see the Commissioner of Police.

"This is a surprise," he informed Anderton, holding out his small gray-gloved hand. "It was my impression you had been taken in by the acting Commissioner."

"I'm still out," Anderton answered shortly, shaking hands. "After all, Witwer has that same reel of tape." He indicated the package Kaplan clutched in his steely fingers and met the man's gaze confidently.

In spite of his nervousness, General Kaplan was in good humor. "This is a great occasion for the Army," he revealed. "You'll be glad to hear I'm going to give the public a full account of the spurious charge brought against you."

"Fine," Anderton answered noncommittally.

"It will be made clear that you were unjustly accused." General Kaplan was trying to discover what Anderton knew. "Did Fleming have an opportunity to acquaint you with the situation?"

"To some degree," Anderton replied. "You're going to read only the minority report? That's all you've got there?"

"I'm going to compare it to the majority report." General Kaplan signalled an aide and a leather briefcase was produced.

"Everything is here—all the evidence we need," he said. "You don't mind being an example, do you? Your case symbolizes the unjust arrests of countless individuals." Stiffly, General Kaplan examined his wristwatch. "I must begin. Will you join me on the platform?"

"Why?"

Coldly, but with a kind of repressed vehemence, General Kaplan said: "So they can see the living proof. You and I to-gether—the killer and his victim. Stand-ing side by side, exposing the whole sinister fraud which the police have been operating."

"Gladly," Anderton agreed. "What are we waiting for?"

Disconcerted, General Kaplan moved toward the platform. Again, he glanced uneasily at Anderton, as if visibly wonder-ing why he had appeared and what he really knew. His uncertainty grew as Anderton willingly mounted the steps of the platform and found himself a seat directly beside the speaker's podium.

"You fully comprehend what I'm going to be saying?" General Kaplan demanded. "The exposure will have considerable repercussions. It may cause the Senate to reconsider the basic validity of the Pre-crime system."

"I understand," Anderton answered, arms folded. "Let's go."

A hush had descended on the crowd. But there was a restless, eager stirring when General Kaplan obtained the brief-case and began arranging his material in front of him.

"The man sitting at my side," he began, in a clean, clipped voice, "is familiar to you all. You may be surprised to see him, for until recently he was described by the police as a dangerous killer."

The eyes of the crowd focused on Anderton. Avidly, they peered at the only potential killer they had ever been privi-leged to see at close range.

"Within the last few hours, however," General Kaplan continued, "the police order for his arrest has been cancelled; because former Commissioner Anderton voluntarily gave himself up? No, that is not strictly accurate. He is sitting here. He has not given himself up, but the police are no longer interested in him. John Allison Anderton is innocent of any crime in the past, present, and future. The allegations against him were patent frauds, diabolical distortions of a contaminated penal system based on a false premise—a vast, impersonal engine of destruction grinding men and women to their doom."

Fascinated, the crowd glanced from Kaplan to Anderton. Everyone was familiar with the basic situation.

"Many men have been seized and imprisoned under the so-called prophylactic Precrime structure," General Kaplan continued, his voice gaining feeling and strength. "Accused not of crimes they have

committed, *but of crimes they will commit.*
It is asserted that these men, if allowed to
remain free, will at some future time commit felonies."

"But there can be no valid knowledge
about the future. As soon as precognitive
information is obtained, *it cancels itself
out.* The assertion that this man will commit a future crime is paradoxical. The very
act of possessing this data renders it spurious. In every case, without exception, the
report of the three police precogs has
invalidated their own data. If no arrests
had been made, there would still have
been no crimes committed."

Anderton listened idly, only half-hearing
the words. The crowd, however, listened
with great interest. General Kaplan was
now gathering up a summary made from
the minority report. He explained what it
was and how it had come into existence.

From his coat pocket, Anderton slipped
out his gun and held it in his lap. Already,
Kaplan was laying aside the minority

report, the precognitive material obtained from "Jerry." His lean, bony fingers groped for the summary of first, "Donna," and after that, "Mike."

"This was the original majority report," he explained. "The assertion, made by the first two precogs, that Anderton would commit a murder. Now here is the automatically invalidated material. I shall read it to you." He whipped out his rimless glasses, fitted them to his nose, and started slowly to read.

A queer expression appeared on his face. He halted, stammered, and abruptly broke off. The papers fluttered from his hands. Like a cornered animal, he spun, crouched, and dashed from the speaker's stand.

For an instant his distorted face flashed past Anderton. On his feet now, Anderton raised the gun, stepped quickly forward, and fired. Tangled up in the rows of feet projecting from the chairs that filled the platform, Kaplan gave a single shrill shriek of agony and fright. Like a ruined bird, he tumbled, fluttering and flailing, from the platform to the ground below. Anderton stepped to the railing, but it was already over.

Kaplan, as the majority report had asserted, was dead. His thin chest was a smoking cavity of darkness, crumbling ash that broke loose as the body lay twitching.

Sickened, Anderton turned away, and moved quickly between the rising figures of stunned Army officers. The gun, which he still held, guaranteed that he would not be interfered with. He leaped from the platform and edged into the chaotic mass of people at its base. Stricken, horrified, they struggled to see what had happened. The incident, occurring before their very eyes, was incomprehensible. It would take time for acceptance to replace blind terror.

At the periphery of the crowd, Anderton was seized by the waiting police. "You're lucky to get out," one of them whispered to him as the car crept cautiously ahead.

"I guess I am," Anderton replied remotely. He settled back and tried to compose himself. He was trembling and dizzy. Abruptly, he leaned forward and was violently sick.

"The poor devil," one the cops murmured sympathetically.

Through the swirls of misery and nausea, Anderton was unable to tell whether the cop was referring to Kaplan or to himself.

burly policemen assisted Lisa and John Anderton in the packing and loading of their possessions. In fifty years, the ex-Commissioner of Police had accumulated a vast collection of material goods. Somber and pensive, he stood watching the procession of crates on their way to the waiting trucks.

By truck they would go directly to the field—and from there to Centaurus X by inter-system transport. A long trip for an old man. But he wouldn't have to make it back.

"There goes the second from the last crate," Lisa declared, absorbed and preoccupied by the task. In sweater and slacks, she roamed through the barren rooms, checking on last-minute details. "I suppose we won't be able to use these new atronic appliances. They're still using electricity on Centten."

"I hope you don't care too much," Anderton said.

"We'll get used to it," Lisa replied, and gave him a fleeting smile. "Won't we?"

"I hope so. You're positive you'll have no regrets. If I thought—"

"No regrets," Lisa assured him. "Now suppose you help me with this crate."

○ ○ ○ ○ ○ ○

As they boarded the lead truck, Witwer drove up in a patrol car. He leaped out and hurried up to them, his face looking

STRANGELY

strangely haggard. "Before you take off," he said to Anderton, "you'll have to give me a break-down on the situation with the precogs. I'm getting inquiries from the Senate. They want to find out if the middle report, the retraction, was an error—or what." Confusedly, he finished: "I still can't explain it. The minority report was wrong, wasn't it?"

"Which minority report?" Anderton inquired, amused.

Witwer blinked. "Then that *is* it. I might have known."

Seated in the cabin of the truck, Anderton got out his pipe and shook tobacco into it. With Lisa's lighter he ignited the tobacco and began operations. Lisa had gone back to the house, wanting to be sure nothing vital had been overlooked.

"There were three minority reports," he told Witwer, enjoying the young man's confusion. Someday, Witwer would learn not to wade into situations he didn't fully understand. Satisfaction was Anderton's final emotion. Old and worn-out as he was, he had been the only one to grasp the real nature of the problem.

"The three reports were consecutive," he explained. "The first was 'Donna.' In that time-path, Kaplan told me of the plot, and I promptly murdered him. 'Jerry,' phased slightly ahead of 'Donna,' used her report as data. He factored in my knowledge of the report. In that, the second time-path, all I wanted to do was to keep my job. It wasn't Kaplan I wanted to kill. It was my own position and life I was interested in."

"And 'Mike' was the third report? That came *after* the minority report?" Witwer corrected himself. "I mean, it came last?"

" 'Mike' was the last of the three, yes. Faced with the knowledge of the first report, I had decided *not* to kill Kaplan. That produced report two. But faced with *that* report, I changed my mind back. Report two, situation two, was the situation Kaplan wanted to create. It was to the advantage of the police to recreate position one. And by that time I was thinking of the police. I had figured out what Kaplan was doing. The third report invalidated the second one in the same way the second one invalidated the first. That brought us back where we started from."

Lisa came over, breathless and gasping. "Let's go—we're all finished here." Lithe and agile, she ascended the metal rungs of the truck and squeezed in beside her husband and the driver. The latter obediently started up his truck and the others followed.

"Each report was different," Anderton concluded. "Each was unique. But two of them agreed on one point. If left free, *I would kill Kaplan.* That created the illusion of a majority report. Actually, that's all it was—an illusion. 'Donna' and 'Mike' previewed the same event—but in two totally different time-paths, occurring under totally different situations. 'Donna' and 'Jerry,' the so-called minority report and half of the majority report, were incorrect. Of the three, 'Mike' was correct—since no report came after his, to invalidate him. That sums it up."

Anxiously, Witwer trotted along beside the truck, his smooth, blond face creased with worry. "Will it happen again? Should we overhaul the set-up?"

"It can happen in only one circumstance," Anderton said. "My case was unique, since I had access to the data. It *could* happen again—but only to the next Police Commissioner. So watch your step." Briefly, he grinned, deriving no inconsiderable comfort from Witwer's strained expression. Beside him, Lisa's red lips twitched and her hand reached out and closed over his.

"Better keep your eyes open," he informed young Witwer. "It might happen to you at any time."

ABOUT THE AUTHOR

ABOUT THE AUTHOR ABOUT THE

AUTHOR. ABOUT

tHE

AUTHOR. ABOUT

tHE AUTHOR

PHILIP K. DICK.. was born in Chicago in 1928 and lived most of his life in California. He briefly attended the University of California, but dropped out before completing any classes. In 1952 he began writing professionally and proceeded to write thirty-six novels and five short story collections. He won the Hugo Award for best novel in 1962 for *The Man in the High Castle* and the John W. Campbell Memorial Award for best novel of the year in 1974 for *Flow My Tears, the Policeman Said.* PHILIP K. DICK.. died of heart failure following a stroke on March 2, 1982, in Santa Ana,

California.

"it's beginning to look as though greatness has been thrust upon Philip K. Dick. . . . [he] has chosen to handle material too nutty to accept, too admonitory to forget, too haunting to abandon." --THE WASHINGTON POST

"A brilliant, idiosyncratic, formidably intelligent writer. . . . He illuminates. He casts light. He gives off a radiance. Philip K. Dick is awe inspiring." --THE WASHINGTON POST

"Philip K. Dick was science fiction's greatest extrapolator of modern angst." --NEW YORK DAILY NEWS

"More than anyone else in the field, Mr. Dick

"... REALLY PUTS YOU INSID[E] PEOPLE'S MINDS." --TH[E] WALL STREET JOURNAL

"DICK [WAS] MANY AUTHORS: A POOR MAN'S PYNCHON, A[N] ORACULAR POSTMODERN, [A] RICH PRODUCT OF THE CHANGING COUNTERCULTURE." -[-] THE VILLAGE VOICE

"DICK IS ENTERTAINING U[S] ABOUT REALITY AND MADNESS, TIME AND DEATH, SI[N] AND SALVATION. . . . WE HAVE OUR OWN HOMEGROW[N] BORGES." --URSULA K. [?] LEGUIN, THE NEW REPUBLIC

"PHILIP K. DICK'S BES[T] BOOKS ALWAYS DESCRIBE [A] FUTURE THAT IS BOTH EN- TIRELY RECOGNIZABLE AN[D] UTTERLY UNIMAGINABLE." -- THE NEW YORK TIMES BOO[K] REVIEW

"PHILIP K. DICK IS ONE OF THE MOST ORIGINAL PRACTI- TIONERS WRITING ANY KIN[D] OF FICTION." --THE SUNDAY TIMES [LONDON]

THE MINORITY REPORT THE[?]

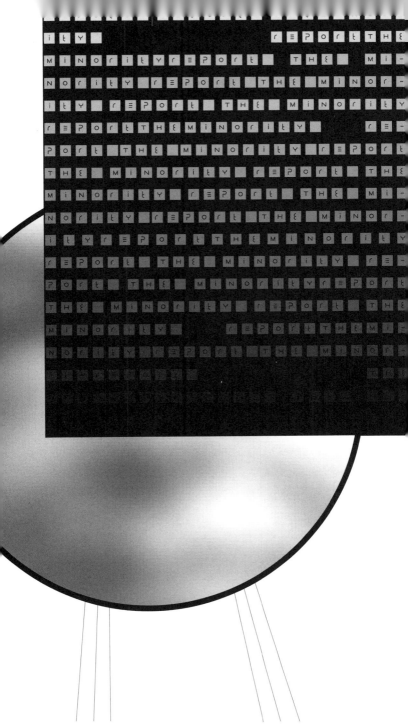

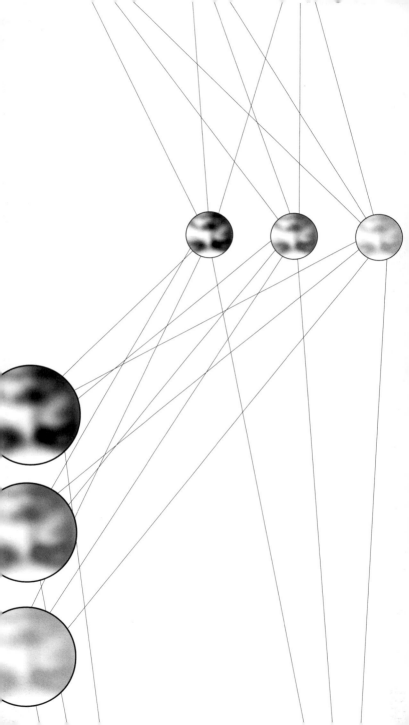